Apple Pay Essentials

Harness the power of Apple Pay in your iOS apps and integrate it with global payment gateways

Ernest Bruce

PUBLISHING

BIRMINGHAM - MUMBAI

Apple Pay Essentials

First published: February 2016

Production reference: 1190216

Published by Packt Publishing Ltd.
Livery Place
35 Livery Street
Birmingham B3 2PB, UK.

ISBN 978-1-78588-638-6

www.packtpub.com

Credits

Author
Ernest Bruce

Reviewer
Zeeshan Chawdhary

Commissioning Editor
Veena Pagare

Acquisition Editor
Kirk D'Costa

Content Development Editor
Preeti Singh

Technical Editor
Siddhesh Patil

Copy Editors
Shruti Iyer
Priyanka Ravi

Project Coordinator
Shweta H Birwatkar

Proofreader
Safis Editing

Indexer
Rekha Nair

Production Coordinator
Aparna Bhagat

Cover Work
Aparna Bhagat

About the Author

Ernest Bruce is an accomplished technical writer and software engineer. He has worked for 13 years at Apple, Inc., where he held the position of Senior Technical Writer writing developer documentation. At Apple, Ernest specialized in writing documentation for the Xcode toolset, focusing on the Xcode user guide, and Xcode overview, as well as unit testing documentation and sample code. He also worked extensively on API documentation for the OS X and iOS platforms. Ernest helped design and develop the Xcode help articles that aid developers in getting around the user interface of the Xcode app. Before his years at Apple, Ernest worked as a programmer for Ping, Inc., where he helped manage the manufacturing processes using APL (A Programming Language). Ernest also has extensive experience in customer service, which has been instrumental to him developing content that readers find clear and easy to read, and that makes complex concepts more approachable.

Ernest is the head of Nerd Brawn, LLC, a software development company that focuses on developing platforms that help people learn about their environment and each other in innovative ways. The company is also working on new techniques to present content on desktop computers, tablets, and mobile phones.

About the Reviewer

Zeeshan Chawdhary has been dabbling with location-based technologies since 2007, having working with industry leaders like Foursquare, Google, and Yahoo in the LBS space. He is been working with startups for the past few years; e-commerce, location-based services, mobile apps – he has built them all, and scaled up for millions of users.

He is also an author, having written three books for Packt Publishing on iOS, Windows Phone, and iBooks Author respectively. He is currently writing another book on Ubuntu and getting his hands dirty with Android.

> I would like to thank Packt Publishing for generously offering me books to review; it not only helps me learn new technologies but helps me strengthen what I know, as well as learn how other programmers work.

www.PacktPub.com

eBooks, discount offers, and more

Did you know that Packt offers eBook versions of every book published, with PDF and ePub files available? You can upgrade to the eBook version at www.PacktPub.com and as a print book customer, you are entitled to a discount on the eBook copy. Get in touch with us at customercare@packtpub.com for more details.

At www.PacktPub.com, you can also read a collection of free technical articles, sign up for a range of free newsletters and receive exclusive discounts and offers on Packt books and eBooks.

https://www2.packtpub.com/books/subscription/packtlib

Do you need instant solutions to your IT questions? PacktLib is Packt's online digital book library. Here, you can search, access, and read Packt's entire library of books.

Why subscribe?

- Fully searchable across every book published by Packt
- Copy and paste, print, and bookmark content
- On demand and accessible via a web browser

Table of Contents

Preface

Whether you are relatively new to iOS app development or a seasoned expert, *Apple Pay Essentials* provides the skills that you need to easily incorporate Apple Pay into the payment workflows of your apps. This book shows you how to obtain the certificates that ensure payment information is securely transmitted between the user's iOS device, your payment gateway, and the banks involved in an Apple Pay transaction. The book teaches you how to provide a simple and consistent user experience, which expedites the time between desire and acquire. You learn how to respond to changes that the user makes to your preconfigured payment sheet, which is where the user confirms or modifies order and payment details. This book guides you through the interactions that your app makes with your payment gateway and your order-processing system. Finally, this book shows you how to design a simple order-processing web app that processes orders and payments submitted by client apps.

What this book covers

Chapter 1, *Getting Started with Apple Pay*, describes how online payments work in general, and it introduces Apple Pay — a simpler and more secure online payment model. This chapter also shows you how to obtain the Apple Pay merchant certificates that ensure that only the appropriate entities have access to sensitive payment information.

Chapter 2, *Payment Request Workflow*, describes how to create a payment request, which is an object that stores information that is critical to payment processing (such as currency and payment network requirements) and details about the customer's order. It also shows you how to manage the main elements of the Apple Pay user experience: the **Apple Pay** button, and the payment sheet. This chapter also explains how to get inventory details from an order-processing web app, and how to present product information to the user.

Chapter 3, Payment Authorization Workflow, shows you how your app should respond to payment sheet events, such as shipping address change, and user authorization of the payment.

Chapter 4, Payment Processing Workflow, describes the actors and operations involved in processing a payment, including your order processing web app.

Chapter 5, Designing an Order Management Server, describes the main components of an order management server, including its data structure, and client API.

Chapter 6, Apple Pay API Summary, summarizes the API that is used for Apple Pay transactions.

What you need for this book

To follow along with the content presented in this book, which is based on the book's example code, you need the hardware and software needed for iOS development: a development Mac, an iOS device that supports Apple Pay, and a recent version of the Xcode developer tools. You need to be able to build apps on your Mac and run them on the iOS device, which requires a wired connection between the computer and the device (so that Xcode can install the app on the device). When running the example app on iOS Simulator, the example app connects to the order management web app running on the computer through a URI that targets the appropriate process. When running the app on the iOS device, however, the connection must be done wirelessly. Therefore, you need to configure your development Mac as a proxy server so that HTTP requests to the order management web app from the iOS device are resolved by the web app on the computer and do not go to the wider network. The documentation in the example code explains how to configure your development Mac as a proxy server using the SquidMan proxy-server software.

Who this book is for

This book is intended for people who want to learn how to incorporate Apple Pay into their iOS apps so that their customers can pay for goods and services quickly and securely. A moderate knowledge of the iOS API and the Xcode developer tools is required.

Conventions

In this book, you will find a number of text styles that distinguish between different kinds of information. Here are some examples of these styles and an explanation of their meaning.

Code words in text, database table names, folder names, filenames, file extensions, pathnames, dummy URLs, user input, and Twitter handles are shown as follows: "Enter the identifier string in the ID field — for example, `merchant.com.company.merchantapp`."

A block of code is set as follows:

```
PKContact contact= [PKContact new];
contact.phoneNumber=
  [CNPhoneNumber phoneNumberWithStringValue: @"678-555-1234"];
```

When we wish to draw your attention to a particular part of a code block, the relevant lines or items are set in bold:

```
- (void) paymentAuthorizationViewControllerDidFinish:
         (PKPaymentAuthorizationViewController*) controller
{
    [self dismissViewControllerAnimated:true completion:nil];
}
```

New terms and **important words** are shown in bold. Words that you see on the screen, for example, in menus or dialog boxes, appear in the text like this: "Under **iOS Apps**, click on **Identifiers**."

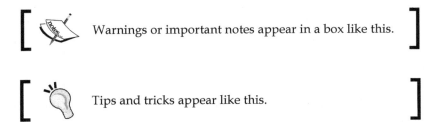

[Warnings or important notes appear in a box like this.]

[Tips and tricks appear like this.]

Reader feedback

Feedback from our readers is always welcome. Let us know what you think about this book—what you liked or disliked. Reader feedback is important for us as it helps us develop titles that you will really get the most out of.

To send us general feedback, simply e-mail feedback@packtpub.com, and mention the book's title in the subject of your message.

If there is a topic that you have expertise in and you are interested in either writing or contributing to a book, see our author guide at www.packtpub.com/authors.

Customer support

Now that you are the proud owner of a Packt book, we have a number of things to help you to get the most from your purchase.

Downloading the example code

You can download the example code files from your account at http://www.packtpub.com for all the Packt Publishing books you have purchased. If you purchased this book elsewhere, you can visit http://www.packtpub.com/support and register to have the files e-mailed directly to you.

Errata

Although we have taken every care to ensure the accuracy of our content, mistakes do happen. If you find a mistake in one of our books—maybe a mistake in the text or the code—we would be grateful if you could report this to us. By doing so, you can save other readers from frustration and help us improve subsequent versions of this book. If you find any errata, please report them by visiting http://www.packtpub.com/submit-errata, selecting your book, clicking on the **Errata Submission Form** link, and entering the details of your errata. Once your errata are verified, your submission will be accepted and the errata will be uploaded to our website or added to any list of existing errata under the Errata section of that title.

To view the previously submitted errata, go to https://www.packtpub.com/books/content/support and enter the name of the book in the search field. The required information will appear under the **Errata** section.

Piracy

Piracy of copyrighted material on the Internet is an ongoing problem across all media. At Packt, we take the protection of our copyright and licenses very seriously. If you come across any illegal copies of our works in any form on the Internet, please provide us with the location address or website name immediately so that we can pursue a remedy.

Please contact us at copyright@packtpub.com with a link to the suspected pirated material.

We appreciate your help in protecting our authors and our ability to bring you valuable content.

Questions

If you have a problem with any aspect of this book, you can contact us at questions@packtpub.com, and we will do our best to address the problem.

1
Getting Started with Apple Pay

Apple Pay is a mobile payment system that lets iPhone users pay for goods and services using Touch ID. Instead of entering or confirming payment card information (credit or debit card) every time they make a purchase, users can authorize payment for items securely by touching the Home button. It is important to note that during an Apple Pay transaction, payment card information never leaves the user's phone; this information is stored securely in the device. Instead, a payment token stores all the information you need to process the payment all the way from authorization to settlement (that is, when the user's funds are transferred to your merchant bank account).

Using Apple Pay, you do not have to store your customers' payment card information on your servers. This helps reduce your customers' misgivings about paying for goods within your app; they trust that their payment card information is secure in their devices. You benefit by not having to deal with payment card information at all, at least not for Apple Pay-based transactions. (When a user's device does not support Apple Pay, or the user has not yet added payment cards to the device, you may have to process payment using regular means, which may involve capturing and storing payment card information.)

Although you are freed from storing payment card details on your systems, you still have to deal with processing the payments, either directly or through a payment gateway. In either case, you need to get an Apple Pay merchant identifier and certificate to decrypt the payment token that Apple Pay creates with a transaction's payment information. To use Apple Pay in your app, you need to enable the Apple Pay capability in your project, which requires the Apple Pay merchant identifier.

This chapter describes how online payments work, online payments being a web-centric version of the traditional **Electronic Draft Capture** (EDC) system used to process credit card transactions. You will also learn the basics of the Apple Pay payment workflow, starting with displaying the **Apple Pay** button when Apple Pay is available on the user's device, presenting the Apple Pay payment sheet, and processing the transaction on your servers.

This chapter will do the following:

- Provide an overview of the online payment process
- Introduce the Apple Pay payment workflow
- Show you how to create an Apple Pay merchant identifier and certificate
- Describe how to turn on the Apple Pay capability for an app in Xcode

An overview of the online payment process

Customers usually carry payment cards (debit or credit cards) in purses or wallets, which they use to pay for goods and services. When a cardholder pays a merchant with a payment card, the merchant usually uses a payment gateway to process the payment. A payment gateway is an e-commerce service that authorizes payment card-based transactions. The *payment gateway* performs several tasks to process the transaction, but it's its main task is the encryption of payment card information before submitting the transaction for authorization to a payment processor. A *payment processor* interacts with the bank that issued the customer's card (known as the *issuing bank* or *issuer*) that ultimately authorizes or declines the transaction. The payment processor may be implemented by the payment gateway, a third party, or the merchant. A merchant would implement a custom payment processor to, for example, integrate with a custom inventory and ordering system.

Merchants that do not manage inventory may deal only with a payment gateway. Payment gateways provide libraries or frameworks that apps can link to. When processing a payment, the app hands off a payment token to the library, which processes the payment and returns the result (*authorized* or *declined*) to the app. The gateway performs all the tasks necessary to authorize the transaction and transfer the payment amount from the card issuer to the merchant's acquiring bank. The *acquiring bank* (also known as the *acquirer*) is the bank that receives the cardholder's payments and credits them to the merchant's bank account (which is a special type of account used to receive payment from payment cards, also known as a *merchant account*).

Merchants that need to integrate with custom ordering and inventory management systems need a more hands-on approach to payment processing. This is the scenario discussed in this book.

First, let's talk about how online payment systems work. The payment process takes place in two phases:

- Authorization
- Settlement

In a successful authorization, an *authorization hold* is placed on the customer's card, reserving the funds that finance the transaction. Later, the merchant consumes or settles the transaction to transfer the funds from the customer's card into the merchant's account.

The following steps describe the authorization process:

1. The customer presents a payment card to pay for a product or service.

2. The merchant encrypts the card's information and sends an authorization request to the payment gateway.

3. The payment gateway then forwards the authorization request to the payment processor.

4. The payment processor forwards the authorization request to the appropriate payment card association (Visa, MasterCard, American Express, Discover, and so on).

5. The card association forwards the authorization request to the issuing bank, which ultimately approves or declines the transaction. Some card associations, such as Discover and American Express, are also issuing banks.

6. The issuing bank receives the authorization request from the payment processor and sends its response (*authorized* or *declined*) to the payment processor. The issuing bank then holds a *transaction authorization* or authorization hold that links the merchant, payment card, and amount approved (the funds are reserved but not debited from the cardholder's account).

7. The payment processor forwards the issuing bank's response to the payment gateway.

8. The payment gateway, in turn, forwards the response to the merchant, who relays the information to the cardholder.

Either immediately, or at the end of the day, the merchant starts the *settlement* process to receive the funds. This process is similar to the procedure used to request the payment authorization; however, instead of authorizing the transaction, the issuing bank moves the authorization hold to a debit and prepares the transaction for settlement with the acquiring bank:

1. The merchant submits the approved authorization to its acquiring bank through the payment processor.
2. The acquiring bank makes a settlement request to the issuing bank.
3. The issuing bank makes a settlement payment to the acquiring bank.
4. The acquiring bank deposits the approved amount into the merchant's bank account.

The Apple Pay payment workflow

If you develop an app that is capable of interacting with a payment gateway to process payment cards, you or your company is a *merchant*, and the app is a *merchant app*.

This is an overview of the payment workflow:

1. **Present the Apple Pay button**: Present this button only if the user can make Apple Pay payments.
2. **Create the payment request**: This request contains essential payment information and details about the order.
3. **Present the payment sheet**: This sheet presents order information that the user can modify, such as shipping information.
4. **Respond to changes by the user**: As the user makes changes, update items such as shipping costs and discounts.
5. **Submit payment information to payment gateway**: When the user authorizes the payment request, submit the payment and order information to the appropriate systems.

Presenting the Apple Pay button

When a user reaches a screen in your app that lets the user purchase something, the app should present the **Apple Pay** button (if the user can use Apple Pay on the device) so that the user can tap the button, verify the purchase details, and authorize the app through Touch ID to complete the order and charge the order amount to the appropriate payment card. Deciding whether the user can use Apple Pay involves two steps:

- Determining whether the device supports Apple Pay
- Determining whether the user has added payment cards that you support to the device

 Your app must make both checks before displaying the **Apple Pay** button. If either check fails, the app must not present the **Apple Pay** button. Instead, it should offer a traditional payment method (such as obtaining a credit card number and a shipping address) through a Buy button.

Creating the payment request

If the user can use Apple Pay, your app prepares a payment request. A *payment request* is an object that describes the items to charge for, the card associations that you support, and billing and shipping information.

The main components of a payment request are *payment summary items*, which describe the payment request to the user. A payment summary item represents a component of the transaction, such as the subtotal, a discount, shipping cost, tax, and the grand total. Each item has a label that describes what each amount means. The last item is the most important because it identifies the payee and the debit amount that the user will see in the next payment card statement. Therefore, this item should have your company's name as its label.

In addition to the payment summary items, your app sets properties of the payment request that describe which card associations and online payment protocols you support. Your app must support at least the 3D Secure protocol. The **EMV (Europay, MasterCard, and Visa)** protocol is optional.

The payment request also lets you indicate that you want the user to specify particular order details, such as shipping or billing information. For example, you may require an e-mail or postal address.

If your ordering system requires additional information, such as the order number, you can include this information in the payment request as custom application data. Apple Pay includes a hash of this information in the payment token you receive when the user authorizes the payment. If your ordering system requires this information later, your app must be able to provide it separately.

Presenting the payment sheet

Once your app creates the payment request and the user taps the **Apple Pay** button, the app presents a payment sheet to the user. The *payment sheet* (formally known as the *payment authorization view controller*) presents the payment summary items in the payment request to the user for review. The user can change aspects of the order before authorizing payment. The user may also decide not to purchase the goods and cancel the transaction.

Responding to order changes and payment authorization

Your app implements a delegate of the payment sheet to respond to the user's actions by, for example, updating the order shipping cost and grand total when the user chooses a different shipping method.

When the user authorizes the payment request with Touch ID, Apple Pay interacts with the device's secure element (the chip that securely stores payment card details on the device, details that not even Apple has access to) and Apple's servers to generate a one-time-use payment token. The *payment information* describes the payment transaction and contains all the information needed to charge the payment amount to the user's payment card (but this does not contain card numbers).

Apple encrypts the information in the token on its servers using your merchant certificate.

Submitting the payment information to the payment gateway

When the payment sheet tells its delegate that the user has authorized the payment request and sends the user the payment information, the delegate calls a synchronous method that forwards the payment information to your payment gateway. When the method returns, it provides the delegate with the result of the payment request. If the payment request is approved, the payment sheet displays a confirmation to the user that the transaction is approved and informs its delegate. The delegate then dismisses the payment sheet and displays a custom confirmation screen; such a screen may display the order number and a *thank you* message. If the payment request is not approved, the delegate must display an appropriate screen and ask the user for another form of payment.

Enabling Apple Pay in your app

For your app to be able to use Apple Pay, you must have an Apple merchant identifier and merchant certificate. Apple uses the certificate to encrypt payment information in the payment token. Your payment gateway (Stripe, Worldpay, and so on) uses the certificate to decrypt information in the payment token.

Creating your app's Apple Pay merchant identifier

You must have access to your team's **Member Center** portal and your payment gateway's certificate management facilities.

Create your merchant identifier in your team's **Member Center** page through the following steps:

1. In **Member Center**, click on **Certificates, Identifiers & Profiles**.
2. Under **iOS Apps**, click on **Identifiers**.
3. Under **Identifiers**, click on **Merchant IDs**.
4. Click on **Continue** (if this is your first merchant identifier) or on the plus sign (+) button in the upper-right corner of the page.

5. Enter a description for the merchant identifier in the **Description** field, for example `MerchantApp merchant identifier`.

6. Enter the identifier string in the ID field, for example `merchant.com.company.merchantapp`.

7. Click on **Continue** and then click on **Register**.

8. Click on **Done**.

Request an Apple Pay certificate from your payment gateway by performing the following:

1. In your payment gateway's certificate management page, create an Apple Pay certificate.

2. Download the **Certificate Signing Request (CSR)** file to your Mac.

Now, follow these steps to create your app merchant certificate in Member Center:

1. In the **Certificates, Identifiers & Profiles** page, under **iOS Apps**, under **Certificates**, click on **All**.

2. Then, select **Apple Pay Certificate** and click on **Continue**.

3. Under **Which Merchant ID would you like to use?**, select the appropriate merchant identifier and click on **Continue**.

4. Under **Generate your certificate**, click on **Choose File**.

5. Choose the CSR file you obtained from your payment gateway.

6. Next, click on **Generate** and then click on **Download** to download your app merchant certificate to your Mac.

Upload your app merchant certificate to your payment gateway via the following steps:

1. In your payment gateway's certificate management page, upload the merchant certificate you downloaded from the **Member Center** portal.

2. Confirm that your merchant certificate is listed in your payment gateway account.

Installing your app's Apple Pay merchant certificate on your Mac

Double-click on the merchant certificate you downloaded earlier from **Member Center**. **Keychain Access** will then open and install the certificate along with your other certificates.

Enabling Apple Pay in your app's Xcode project

To provide your app with access to Apple Pay, you need to turn on the Apple Pay capability in the Xcode project. Perform the following:

1. First, open your project in Xcode.
2. Select the target that builds the app to open the target editor.
3. Then, click on **Capabilities**.
4. Find the **Apple Pay** capability and toggle the corresponding switch to its on position.
5. In the dialog that appears, select the appropriate development team, and click on **Choose**.

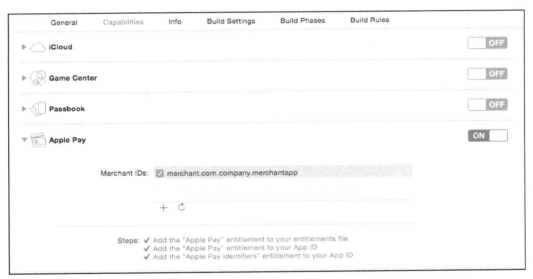

xcode-turn_on_apple_pay-done.png

Summary

In this chapter, you learned about the online payment process followed by merchants to obtain card-based payments. The chapter introduced general online payment concepts to describe how an app uses Apple Pay to perform a similar function but more securely. Finally, you learned how to create the Apple Pay merchant identifier and merchant certificate to enable Apple Pay payment in your apps.

The next chapter focuses on the payment request workflow, where you present the **Apple Pay** button when Apple Pay is available on the device, create the payment request, and present the payment sheet based on that request.

2
Payment Request Workflow

When your customer decides to purchase an item that is offered in your app, it is your responsibility to give the user a smooth, fast, and pain-free payment experience. Thankfully, Apple has taken the brunt of this effort by implementing Apple Pay. Users do not have to dig up their credit cards and enter shipping addresses to complete an order, even if it is the first time that they use your app. By asking only for the information that is strictly necessary to perform a transaction, you provide your customers with a compelling purchasing experience, which will encourage subsequent purchases from your app.

This chapter describes the things that your app needs to do to give its users a pleasant shopping experience, one in which the barrier between desiring something and having this product shipped to your doorstep is reduced to the gentle touch of a smooth, round button. At the same time, you reduce or eliminate the need to ask for and store your customers' payment information, which is a sensible approach in light of the notable increase in breaches of computer systems to obtain information on active payment cards. You will probably also welcome the marked increase in purchases from the same customers who, in addition to having a better purchasing experience than the ones offered by other apps, have confidence that their payment information will not be compromised (because their card information is not stored in their phones). Having a seamless payment experience will place your app high in its users' list of *loved* and *highly liked* apps, and apps that they would readily recommend to their family and friends.

This chapter covers the following topics:

- Providing an overview of a simple inventory web service that provides inventory information to its clients
- Describing the implementation of a product card that displays essential product information and either an **Apple Pay** button or a regular **Buy** button depending on the availability of Apple Pay on the user's device

- Walking through the process of creating a payment request and displaying a payment sheet with order information for the user to authorize payment (when Apple Pay is available)

Getting information from an inventory service

If users of your app can purchase tangible goods through it, then the app must get information about the availability of such products. One way to accomplish this is through a *web service*. A web service is an app (web app or web process) that runs on a web server and to which clients (desktop or mobile apps) can connect to access resources such as an inventory, product images, orders, and payments. The most web-centric way to access such resources is through the use of *RESTful API*. **Representational State Transfer (REST)** provides a way for a computer to communicate with other computers, akin to the way people browse the web.

When you visit a web page, the page will likely offer options (links) that you can use to access content that is related to this page or the workflow (transaction) in which you are engaged. You then analyze each link to decide which related page to go to next. The RESTful API provides clients with an organic way to interact with resources that are hosted by web servers. Instead of having to follow a rigid API that is dictated by the web service, clients can ask for specific representations of a resource (a browser may ask for its XHTML version, while an iOS app may ask for JavaScript Object Notation or JSON). Embedded in the resource are links to related resources or to operations that modify the state of the resource. For example, after creating an order, the web server may provide links to operations that return the state of this order, modify it, or cancel it. This type of interaction is known as *hypermedia*. Hypermedia refers to the way distributed systems operate, accessing resources by their unique identifiers through a small set of HTTP verbs, such as POST, PUT, GET, and DELETE. This simple communication style provides great flexibility to distributed systems in establishing specialized-communication protocols.

The example solution (iOS app and web service) described in this book (and available for download) makes use of RESTful API to provide access to inventory, orders, and payments. By basing the app's interaction with its web service on a simple RESTful API, we can focus our attention on the main aspects of incorporating Apple Pay in your app and processing payments on your web server.

Before your app can present product information to your customers, it must get this information from your web servers. Shipping information is also important because the shipping methods that you offer may change from time to time, and the app should also get this information regularly. The app would present the shipping methods that are available on the payment sheet to let the user accept the default shipping method or change it. The following sections describe how the example solution gets inventory and shipping information from a web server to the user's device.

Getting inventory information

The example app is very simple. On launch, it requests two things from the web server: the inventory, and the shipping methods that are available. Then, it displays the inventory in a list, as in the following screenshot:

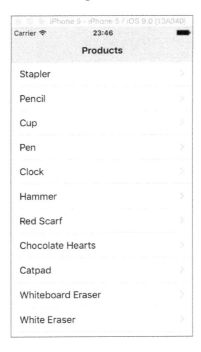

To get the inventory information, the app requests a representation of the resource from the server using a REST API. The resource is found by accessing the `http://red:12345/inventory` **Uniform Resource Identifier** (**URI**). After receiving the data, the app uses the `NSJSONSerialization` class to convert the data that is received (encoded in JSON) into an `NSDictionary` instance, which is the data source for the table (a `UITableView` instance) whose rows display the name of each product in inventory.

This listing shows the model that is used by the web service (implemented in Node.js), the Objective-C class that defines the corresponding iOS model, and the code that converts the JSON into the products dictionary:

```
// Web service JavaScript
var Product_schema= new Schema({
    name:              String,
    description:       String,
    image_uri:         String,
    quantity_on_hand:  Number,
    price:             String
});

// Product.h
@interface Product : NSObject
@property NSString*  name;
@property NSString*  description;
@property NSString*  image_uri;
@property NSUInteger quantity_on_hand;
@property NSString*  price;
@end

// ProductList.m
@interface ProductList ()
@property (nonatomic) NSArray* products;           // array of Product*
@end
@implementation ProductList
- (void) viewDidLoad
{
    [super viewDidLoad];
    self.title= @"Products";

    RestIO* rest_io= [RestIO sharedRestIO];
    [rest_io getResourceAtURI:@"http://red:12345/inventory"
                   completion:^(NSURLResponse* response, NSData* data)
{
```

```objc
    if ([response.MIMEType isEqualToString:@"application/json"])
    {
        NSError* error;
        NSDictionary* json_data= [NSJSONSerialization
JSONObjectWithData:data

options:0

error:&error];
        NSMutableArray* products= [NSMutableArray new];
        for (NSDictionary* json_product in json_data)
        {
            Product* product=     [Product new];
            product.name=         json_product[@"name"];
            product.description=  json_product[@"description"];
            product.image_uri=    json_product[@"image_uri"];
            product.price=        json_product[@"price"];
            {
                NSInteger quantity= [(NSString*)json_
product[@"quantity_on_hand"]
                                                integerValue];
                product.quantity_on_hand= quantity > 0? quantity : 0;
            }
            [products addObject:(NSString*)product];
        }
        _products= products.copy;
        dispatch_async(dispatch_get_main_queue(), ^{
            [(UITableView*)self.view reloadData];
        });
    }
}];
}
...
@end
```

An important thing to note is that a product's price is stored as a string, not a number. This is because performing financial computations with numeric types does not produce accurate results. When performing financial computations, especially those having to do with Apple Pay transactions, you must use instances of the NSDecimalNumber class, which facilitate the accurate computation of arithmetic operations on base-10 numbers. The NSDecimalNumber class also has methods that convert numeric strings to decimal numbers.

Getting shipping information

To provide available shipping methods to customers on the payment sheet, the app needs to get the list from the server. In the sample code, the app's `AppDelegate` object gets this list in its `application:didFinishLaunchingWithOptions:` method.

This listing shows the Node.js and Objective-C model classes of instances of the `ShippingService` class, and the code that gets the shipping services from the server:

```
// Web service JavaScript
var ShippingService_schema= new Schema({
    name:         String,
    description:  String,
    transit_days: Number,
    price:        String
});

// ShippingMethod.h
@interface ShippingService : NSObject
@property NSString*  name;
@property NSString*  detail;
@property NSNumber*  transit_days;
@property NSString*  price;
@end

// AppDelegate.m
#import "AppDelegate.h"
#import "Stripe.h"
#import "RestIO.h"
#import "ShippingMethod.h"

@interface AppDelegate ()
@property (readwrite) NSArray<ShippingMethod*>* shipping_methods;
@end

@implementation AppDelegate
- (BOOL)              application:(UIApplication*) app
  didFinishLaunchingWithOptions:(NSDictionary*)  options
{
    _ApplePay_merchant_identifier= ApplePay_merchant_identifier;
    _ApplePay_supported_networks= @[PKPaymentNetworkVisa,
PKPaymentNetworkAmex, PKPaymentNetworkDiscover,
PKPaymentNetworkPrivateLabel];

    [Stripe setDefaultPublishableKey:StripePublishableKey];
```

```objc
    _rest_io_host= @"http://red:12345";

    // get shipping methods from server
    {
        NSString* shipping_methods_uri= [NSString
stringWithFormat:@"%@%@",_rest_io_host, @"/shipping_methods"];

        RestIO* rest_io= [RestIO sharedRestIO];
        [rest_io getResourceAtURI:shipping_methods_uri
completion:^(NSURLResponse* response, NSData* data) {
            if ([response.MIMEType isEqualToString:@"application/json"])
            {
                NSError* error;
                NSDictionary*   json_data=           [NSJSONSerialization
JSONObjectWithData:data options:0 error:&error];
                NSMutableArray* shipping_methods= [NSMutableArray array];
                for (NSDictionary* json_shipping_method in json_data)
                {
                    ShippingMethod* shipping_method=    [ShippingMethod
new];
                    {
                        shipping_method.name=           json_shipping_
method[@"name"];
                        shipping_method.detail=         json_shipping_
method[@"description"];
                        shipping_method.transit_days= [NSNumber
numberWithShort:[(NSString*)json_shipping_method[@"transit_days"]

integerValue]];
                        shipping_method.price=          json_shipping_
method[@"price"];
                    }

                    [shipping_methods addObject:(NSString*)shipping_
method];
                }
                _shipping_methods= shipping_methods.copy;
            }
        }];
    }
    return YES;
}
...
@end
```

Similar to the `Product` class that was introduced earlier, the `ShippingMethod` class uses a string to store the price of each shipping method. This is because shipping-method prices are added to the price of other items in the payment request, and all these additions must be done using decimal numbers (the `NSDecimalNumber` instances).

Now that the app has the inventory of available products and the shipping methods available to its users, it can show a *product information card* when the user selects a product from the product list and a payment sheet when the user taps the **Apple Pay** button.

Displaying the product card

The Apple Pay user experience starts with the appearance of the **Apple Pay** button. When your customer sees this button, they know that the product pictured on their device's screen can be at their doorstep with as few as two taps. There really is no *step 3.*

The *product card* is a screen that displays product information, such as the product's name, description, and price, and the **Apple Pay** button when Apple Pay is available on the user's device. When Apple Pay is not available (either because the customer's device does not support it or because the customer has not set up Apple Pay on that device), your app should not display the **Apple Pay** button. Instead, it should display either an **Add to Cart** button or a regular **Buy** button, and process the payment using traditional means.

The following sections describe how to design a product-card screen and how to lay out an **Apple Pay** button at runtime when Apple Pay is available.

Presenting product information

The product-card definition starts in the app's main storyboard file, as in the following screenshot:

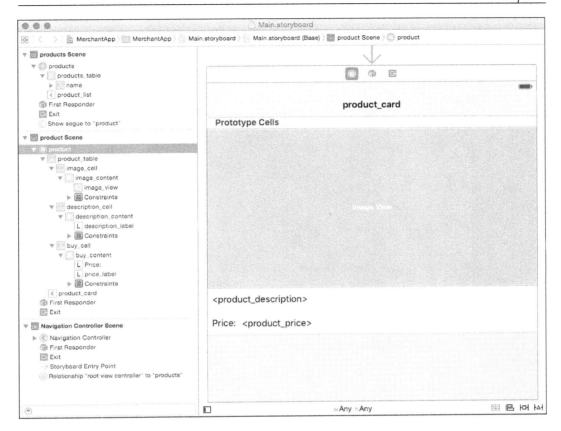

The product scene lays out the elements that make up the product card. This is mainly an image view that displays the product's image and three labels that display the product description, the **Price**: legend, and the product price using a currency formatter.

This listing shows the `viewDidLoad` method of the `ProductCard` object:

```
// ProductCard.m
- (void) viewDidLoad
{
    [super viewDidLoad];

    _currency_formatter=                    [NSNumberFormatter new];
    _currency_formatter.numberStyle= NSNumberFormatterCurrencyStyle;

    // get last-used shipping method
```

```objc
    _shipping_method_name= [[NSUserDefaults standardUserDefaults]
objectForKey:Default_shipping_method_name];

    // define table sections
    {
        short   i= 0;
        sections[  i].cell_row_height=   44; sections[i].cell_type=
ProductDescription;
        sections[++i].cell_row_height=  400; sections[i].cell_type=
ProductImage;
        sections[++i].cell_row_height=   44; sections[i].cell_type=
ProductBuy;
        _section_count= ++i;
    }


    // download product image
    RestIO* rest_io= [RestIO sharedRestIO];
    [rest_io downloadResourceWithURI: _product.image_uri
                      completion: ^
        (NSURL* destination_url)
        {
            dispatch_async(dispatch_get_main_queue(), ^
                {
                    UIImage *image= [UIImage imageWithContentsOfFile:[dest
ination_url path]];
                    [((ProductCard_TableView*)self.view)
setProductImage:image];
                }
            );
        }
    ];

    // get shipping methods
    {
        AppDelegate*    app_delegate=      [UIApplication
sharedApplication].delegate;
        NSMutableArray<PKShippingMethod*>* pk_shipping_methods=
[NSMutableArray new];
        for (ShippingMethod* shipping_method in app_delegate.shipping_
methods)
        {
            PKShippingMethod* pk_shipping_method=
            [PKShippingMethod
             summaryItemWithLabel:[@"Shipping " stringByAppendingString:s
hipping_method.name]
```

```
            amount:[NSDecimalNumber decimalNumberWithString:shipping_
method.price]];
        pk_shipping_method.identifier= shipping_method.name;
        pk_shipping_method.detail=      shipping_method.detail;
        [pk_shipping_methods addObject:pk_shipping_method];
    }
    _pk_shipping_methods= pk_shipping_methods.copy;
  }
}
```

The `viewDidLoad` method instantiates the currency formatter that is used by the *buy* table cell, which displays the product's price and the **Apple Pay** button. However, the **Apple Pay** button is not laid out at design time; it is laid out at run time when the product table displays the buy cell. This setup is explained in the next section.

The `viewDidLoad` method also gets the product's image by getting the resources identified by the product's `image_uri` property. This method uses the REST API to download the image data from the server. When the image is downloaded, the method creates a `UIImage` object, which it assigns to the `view` property of the product table.

Presenting the Apple Pay button

As stated earlier, it is very important that your app does not display the **Apple Pay** button if the user is unable to use Apple Pay on their device. Your app determines whether Apple Pay is available using two methods of the `PKPaymentAuthorizationViewController` class: `canMakePayments`, and `canMakePaymentsUsingNetworks:`.

This listing shows how an example iOS app uses these methods to determine which purchase button to add to the buy cell: the **Apple Pay** button, an instance of the `PKPaymentButton` class, or a **Buy** button implemented as a `UIButton` instance:

```
// ProductCard.m
(ProductCard_BuyCell*) buy_cell
{
    ProductCard_BuyCell* cell=
        (ProductCard_BuyCell*)[(ProductCard_TableView*)self.view dequeue
ReusableCellWithIdentifier:@"buy"];

    NSNumber* price_number= [NSNumber numberWithDouble:[_product.price
doubleValue]];
    cell.price_label.text= [_currency_formatter
stringFromNumber:price_number];
```

```objc
    // determine whether ApplePay is available on this device and is
configured with the accepted payment networks
    BOOL can_use_ApplePay;
    {
        AppDelegate* app_delegate= [UIApplication sharedApplication].
delegate;
        if ((can_use_ApplePay= [PKPaymentAuthorizationViewController
canMakePayments]))
            can_use_ApplePay= [PKPaymentAuthorizationViewController
                                 canMakePaymentsUsingNetworks:app_
delegate.ApplePay_supported_networks];
    }

    // instantiate the purchase button
    UIButton* purchase_button;
    if (can_use_ApplePay)
    // configure a PKPaymentButton (Apple Pay button)
    {
        // create payment button
        purchase_button= [PKPaymentButton buttonWithType:PKPaymentButto
nTypePlain
                                                   style:PKPaymentButton
StyleWhiteOutline];
        purchase_button.tag= ApplePay_button_tag;
    }
    else
    // configure a UIButton
    {
        purchase_button= [UIButton buttonWithType:UIButtonTypeSystem];
        [purchase_button setTitle:@"Buy" forState:UIControlStateNormal];
        purchase_button.tag= Buy_button_tag;
    }

    // define the layout of the purchase button
    ...

    return cell;
}
```

The result of this process is a product card that displays the **Apple Pay** button (if Apple Pay is available on the device), allowing the user to quickly satisfy their impulse to purchase a beautiful product. It is your job to facilitate the satisfaction of this impulse with as few barriers as possible.

When the user taps the **Apple Pay** button, your app starts the Apple Pay transaction by creating a payment request.

Creating the payment request

Now that the user has decided to purchase your product, we are on a mission to help them authorize the payment request with as few distractions and interruptions as possible. A user's attention, especially on a device such as an iPhone, can be fleeting; in the extra second that it takes for them to confirm a billing address (even though they always use the same address), a phone call can come in and, pouf, the sale goes away. Anything you can not show the user helps speed up the authorization. Apple Pay makes this very convenient.

Specifying payment details

The essential components of a payment request (an instance of `PKPaymentRequest`) are: country and currency code, your merchant identifier and capabilities, and the payment networks that you support. You must specify all these properties on each payment request you create.

Country and currency code

You specify these items with the `countryCode` and `currencyCode` properties of the payment request. Specifying these items is important because they identify where and how the payment is processed. The country code is the two-letter code for the country where the payment will be processed (refer to ISO 3166 at `http://www.iso.org/iso/country_codes`). The currency code is the three-letter code that identifies the currency that is used to fund the transaction (refer to ISO 4217 at `http://www.iso.org/iso/home/standards/currency_codes`).

Merchant identifier and capabilities

The Apple merchant identifier is the identifier that you obtained (or will get right now!) from the *Certificates, Identifiers & Profiles* section of the Apple Member Center website. They are reverse-DNS identifiers that start with `merchant.com`. The merchant capabilities identify the payment protocols, 3-D Secure, and EMV (Europay, MasterCard, and Visa). 3-D Secure support is required; EMV support is optional. You specify these components with the `merchantIdentifier` and `merchantCapabilities` properties of the payment request.

This listing shows the code that specifies the payment details of a payment request:

```
// create payment request
PKPaymentRequest *request= [Stripe paymentRequestWithMerchantIdentifie
r:ApplePay_merchant_identifier];
request.merchantIdentifier=          ApplePay_merchant_identifier;
request.countryCode=                 @"US";
request.currencyCode=                @"USD";
request.supportedNetworks=           ApplePay_supported_networks;
request.merchantCapabilities=        PKMerchantCapability3DS;
```

Requiring shipping and billing information

Apple Pay provides all the information that you need to complete a transaction. However, there may be situations in which you need information stored in Apple Pay that is not available to you before the user authorizes the payment request. For example, even though Apple Pay provides shipping and billing information, you may still require that the user enter or confirm the shipping destination before they authorize the payment request to calculate the shipping costs to present in the payment sheet. Keep in mind though that as your customer's billing and shipping details are most likely up to date in Apple Pay, relying on Apple Pay for this information is generally the best approach. Not to mention that by not requiring users to confirm such details, you would be putting them on the fast lane to that magical *authorization touch*.

Requiring shipping or billing addresses

If you need the user to enter shipping or billing information (because your systems interface with other systems that need this information readily), you can specify these requirements with the requiredBillingAddressFields and requiredShippingAddressFields properties of the payment request. For example, to make the billing address a required field, set this property to PKAddressFieldPostalAddress. If you need an e-mail, set it to PKAddressFieldEmail. Finally, to request a name, set the property to PKAddressFieldName. As the values that these properties accept are bitfield constants, you can aggregate them to require multiple items. This listing shows how to require a shipping address and email, and a billing email:

```
// client_app/merchantapp/ProductCard.m
@interface ProductCard()
@property PKPaymentRequest* payment_request;
...
@end

- (void) process_ApplePay_payment_request
{
   // create payment request
   _payment_request=
      [Stripe paymentRequestWithMerchantIdentifier:...];
   {
      // require shipping address and email, and billing email
      _payment_request.requiredShippingAddressFields=
         PKAddressFieldPostalAddress | PKAddressFieldEmail;
      _payment_request.requiredBillingAddressFields=
         PKAddressFieldEmail;
   }
   ...
}
```

Specifying shipping or billing addresses

If your customer has purchased items from your business before, and you have their billing and shipping address, you can prepopulate this information on the payment sheet using the billingAddress and shippingAddress properties of the payment request.

This listing shows how to make shipping and billing information required fields:

```
client_app/merchantapp/ProductCard.m
@interface ProductCard()
```

```
@property PKPaymentRequest* payment_request;
...
@end

- (void) process_ApplePay_payment_request
{
    ...
    // specify a particular shipping address
    PKContact*              contact= [PKContact new];
    CNMutablePostalAddress* address= [CNMutablePostalAddress new];
    address.street=         @"123 Fern Road";
    address.city=           @"San Jose";
    address.postalCode=     @"95123";
    address.country=        @"USA";
    address.ISOCountryCode= @"US";
    contact.postalAddress=  [address copy];

    _payment_request.shippingContact= contact;
    ...
}
```

Specifying shipping methods

If you ship products to your customers, you may offer one or more shipping methods. The example iOS app and web service described earlier shows a basic implementation of such a system. Depending on the size of your enterprise, you may offer shipping methods for particular products or destinations. Regardless of the complexity of the setup, in the payment sheet that you present should be a simple list of shipping methods from which users choose the one that is most convenient to them. The next chapter discusses how to react when the user changes the shipping method in the payment sheet. For now, your focus is on creating an array of shipping methods (the PKShippingMethod instances) to assign to the shippingMethods payment-request property. This listing shows how to create such an array and how to incorporate it on the payment request:

```
// client_app/merchantapp/ProductCard.m
#import "ShippingMethod.h"
...
@property PKPaymentRequest* payment_request;
...
- (void) viewDidLoad
{
    ...
    // get the ShippingMethod objects in the app delegate,
```

```objectivec
    // and convert them to PKShippingMethod objects
    AppDelegate* app_delegate=
        [UIApplication sharedApplication].delegate;
    NSMutableArray<PKShippingMethod*>* pk_shipping_methods=
        [NSMutableArray new];
    for (ShippingMethod* shipping_method in
        app_delegate.shipping_methods)
    {
        PKShippingMethod* pk_shipping_method=
            [PKShippingMethod
                summaryItemWithLabel:
                    [@"Shipping " stringByAppendingString:
                        shipping_method.name]
                amount:
                    [NSDecimalNumber
                        decimalNumberWithString:
                            shipping_method.price]];
        pk_shipping_method.identifier= shipping_method.name;
        pk_shipping_method.detail=     shipping_method.detail;

        [pk_shipping_methods addObject: pk_shipping_method];
    }
    _pk_shipping_methods= pk_shipping_methods.copy;
}

- (void) process_ApplePay_payment_request
{
    // create payment request
    AppDelegate* app_delegate=
        [UIApplication sharedApplication].delegate;
    _payment_request=
        [Stripe paymentRequestWithMerchantIdentifier:
            app_delegate.ApplePay_merchant_identifier];
    ...
    // set the shipping methods
    _payment_request.shippingMethods= _pk_shipping_methods;
    ...
}
```

If, in addition to shipping goods using shipping services, you support in-store pickup of items or special delivery methods, such as for pizza or furniture, then you can specify a list of alternative delivery methods. To specify these shipping types, use the shippingType property of the payment request.

Specifying summary items

The summary items are the elements of the payment sheet that specify the price of the item the user is purchasing, the shipping cost, taxes, discounts, and the total price. Each summary item has a label, such as SHIPPING or TAX. The last item represents the total price with a label, such as PAY ACME. The label of this item must identify your company so that the customer can match the purchase to their payment-card statement. You specify the summary items of a payment request by assigning an array of PKPaymentSummaryItem instances to the paymentSummaryItems property of the payment request. Each summary item has an amount property that represents the cost of the item.

This listing shows how to define the summary items of a payment request:

```
// client_app/merchantapp/ProductCard.m
@property Product*          product;
@property PKPaymentRequest*  payment_request;
@property PKShippingMethod*  selected_shipping_method;
...
// tally the summary items' cost and the grand total
- (NSArray<PKPaymentSummaryItem*>*) computeSummaryItems
{
    NSDecimalNumber* product_price=
        [NSDecimalNumber decimalNumberWithString:_product.price];

    NSDecimalNumber* shipping=
        _selected_shipping_method?
            _selected_shipping_method.amount :
            [NSDecimalNumber zero];

    NSDecimalNumber* tax=
        [product_price decimalNumberByMultiplyingBy:
            [NSDecimalNumber decimalNumberWithString:@"0.08"]];

    NSDecimalNumber* total=
        decimal_number_sum(@[product_price, shipping, tax]);

    // specify summary items
    NSMutableArray<PKPaymentSummaryItem*>* summary_items=
    [NSMutableArray arrayWithArray:
     @[
       [PKPaymentSummaryItem
         summaryItemWithLabel:_product.name amount:product_price],
       [PKPaymentSummaryItem
         summaryItemWithLabel:@"Shipping"    amount:shipping],
```

```
        [PKPaymentSummaryItem
            summaryItemWithLabel:@"Tax"          amount:tax],
        [PKPaymentSummaryItem
            summaryItemWithLabel:@"Acme"         amount:total]
        ]];

    return summary_items.copy;
}

- (void) process_ApplePay_payment_request
{
    // create payment request
    _payment_request=
        [Stripe paymentRequestWithMerchantIdentifier:...];

    // compute summary items and assign them to the payment request
    _payment_request.paymentSummaryItems= [self computeSummaryItems];
    ...
}
```

To specify a summary item representing a discount from the product price, use a negative value for the summary item's amount. When you do not know the value for the amount because the value is generated as part of processing the order, you can indicate this fact to the user by setting the `type` property of the summary item to `PKPaymentSummaryItemTypePending`. This adds an appropriate legend to the item's label.

Specifying custom information tied to the order

If your ordering system needs additional information after the payment has been approved by the issuing bank, you can specify it in the `applicationData` property of the payment request. However, Apple Pay does not deliver this information to you. Your app has to send this information to your system separately.

As part of processing payment, your payment processor gets a hash of the value that you set in the `applicationData` property of the payment request. You can use this hash to verify that the value the app sent separately is the same as the initial value.

Summary

This chapter has shown how your app may obtain data to perform its functions using the REST API, which provides flexible functionality using the standard HTTP idioms (with HTTP verbs such as PUT, GET, UPDATE, and DELETE). It also showed you how to convert this data into information the user can act on, such as product names, descriptions, and images. In particular, this chapter discussed when to present the **Apple Pay** button to the user (only when Apple Pay is available on the user's device). Finally, this chapter walked you through the process of creating a payment request, which includes specifying payment information, such as the Apple merchant identifier and merchant capabilities, shipping and billing information, and the summary items that include the total price of the order labeled with your company name for easy verification with payment-card statements.

Now that the user is looking at the payment sheet, your app needs to respond effectively to changes in the shipping methods or billing and shipping addresses. The ultimate user action though is authorizing the payment request. This is the topic of the next chapter.

3
Payment Authorization Workflow

The *payment sheet* is the most important user-facing aspect of the Apple Pay experience. Also, this is where the user should spend the least amount of time. Your app convinced the user to purchase the product. The payment sheet is where you will take the user from *desire* to *acquire* in as few taps as possible, two taps being the ideal.

In the previous chapter, you learned how to present information in the payment sheet, including a list of the shipping methods you can make available to your customers, and the total price of the order. With the payment sheet up, the user can change the shipping type (from delivery to store pickup, for example), the shipping address, and the payment method (the payment card that will be used to fund the transaction). For each change the user makes, you must update the payment request's summary items to reflect it. For example, when the user changes the shipping method, you must update the summary item that displays the price for shipping the item using the newly selected shipping method.

This chapter shows how to respond to messages from the payment sheet to update the appropriate information on the payment request. It also shows how to start the payment processing workflow in response to the user authorizing the app to submit the payment request for approval by the selected card's issuing bank.

This chapter will do the following:

- Describe the payment authorization workflow
- Demonstrate the implementation of the methods (declared by the payment sheet delegate protocol) that respond to payment sheet messages to update appropriate information in the payment request
- Show you how to dismiss the payment sheet when the user authorizes the payment request or cancels the transaction by tapping the cancel button

Actors and operations in the authorization workflow

The *payment authorization workflow* is a process by which the user confirms or enters the shipping information you provide or request in the payment sheet and authorizes the app to submit the payment request for approval by the issuing bank of the payment card specified in the payment request. The user may also change the payment card to use to fund the payment request, in which case you might need to update the payment request's summary items (by adding surcharges for specific cards, for example).

The payment authorization workflow starts when your app presents the payment sheet (a PKPaymentAuthorizationViewController object) and ends with the user authorizing the payment request. (The user may cancel the transaction by tapping the **Cancel** button on the payment sheet.)

This diagram depicts the actors and operations that are part of the payment authorization workflow:

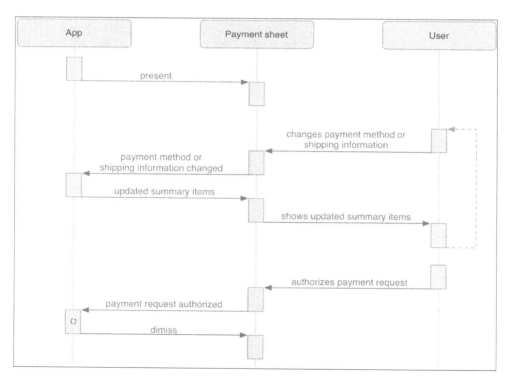

The workflow comprises four steps, as follows:

1. The app presents the payment sheet.
2. The user enters or changes the information you present or require (the less the information shown on the payment sheet, the faster the authorization).
3. The app responds to changes in the payment sheet by updating payment summary items.
4. The user approves the payment request.

These are the operations in more detail:

*   **payment request** (PKPaymentRequest): This is the payment request you use to present the payment sheet.

*   **shipping type** (PKShippingType): This indicates how the customer will get the product being purchased. The available shipping types are delivery (for instance, for office supplies or pizza), store pickup (such as for Apple Watches or jewelry), and service pickup (for example, when you provide transportation or delivery services that offer home pickup). With the store pickup shipping type, you must manage the shipping addresses as they are not shipping addresses but pickup addresses, such as your store's address. For example, in this case, you can set the *shipping* address to your store's address or hide the shipping address by setting the requiredShippingAddressFields property of the payment request to PKAddressFieldNone.

*   **payment summary items** and **shipping method** (PKPaymentSummaryItem, PKShippingMethod): This indicates the summary items displayed after the order's subtotal, including the shipping method selected for the order.

*   **shipping methods** (PKShippingMethod objects): This indicates the shipping methods available to the customer for the order. This list may change if the user changes the shipping address.

*   **payment sheet** (PKPaymentAuthorizationViewController): This is the sheet the app presents to let the user verify or enter the information you require before the user authorizes the payment request. The user authorizes the payment request on this sheet.

*   **payment sheet interaction protocol** (PKPaymentAuthorizationViewControllerDelegate): This is the API the app and the payment sheet use to communicate with each other.

Implementing a shared method to compute summary items

To respond to the delegate method calls from the payment sheet, you should have a single method that computes the payment summary items based on the shipping information. Here's a possible implementation of such a method:

```objc
// client_app/merchantapp/ProductCard.m
@property Product*         product;
@property PKShippingMethod* selected_shipping_method;
...
// tally the summary items' cost and the grand total
- (NSArray<PKPaymentSummaryItem*>*) computeSummaryItems
{
    NSDecimalNumber* product_price=
        [NSDecimalNumber decimalNumberWithString:_product.price];

    NSDecimalNumber* shipping=
        _selected_shipping_method?
          _selected_shipping_method.amount :
          [NSDecimalNumber zero];

    NSDecimalNumber* tax=
        [product_price decimalNumberByMultiplyingBy:
          [NSDecimalNumber decimalNumberWithString:@"0.08"]];

    NSDecimalNumber* total=
        decimal_number_sum(@[product_price, shipping, tax]);

    // specify summary items
    NSMutableArray<PKPaymentSummaryItem*>* summary_items=
    [NSMutableArray arrayWithArray:
     @[
        [PKPaymentSummaryItem
           summaryItemWithLabel: _product.name
                         amount: product_price],
        [PKPaymentSummaryItem
           summaryItemWithLabel: @"Shipping"
                         amount: shipping],
        [PKPaymentSummaryItem
           summaryItemWithLabel: @"Tax"
                         amount: tax],
        [PKPaymentSummaryItem
```

```
            summaryItemWithLabel: @"Acme"
                         amount: total]
    ]];

    return summary_items.copy;
}
```

With this method in place, you can respond to different delegate method calls from the payment sheet and have a consistent algorithm for the computation of the payment summary items.

Responding to user interactions with the payment sheet

After identifying the main actors and operations involved in the payment authorization workflow and with a single method to compute payment summary items, we are ready to delve into your responses to payment sheet messages initiated by the changes the user makes to shipping information.

Note that the correct functionality of the payment sheet is essential to the payment authorization workflow; in particular, the payment sheet must call its delegate methods consistently so that you can correctly gauge when these methods are called as a result of user interaction with the payment sheet. If you use iOS simulators to test your code and notice that the payment sheet delegate methods are not being called, quit and restart the Simulator app.

User changes shipping information

When the user changes the shipping address or contact, your payment sheet delegate receives the `paymentAuthorizationViewController:didSelectShippingContact:completion:` message indicating that the user changed the shipping information for the order.

The new shipping details are encapsulated in a *contact* (a PKContact instance). This contact object contains only the shipping information you requested in the requiredShippingAddressFields property of the payment request. The properties of contact are name, emailAddress, phoneNumber, and postalAddress. So if you required only a postal address and name by setting the requiredShippingAddressFields payment request property to PKAddressField PostalAddress|PKAddressFieldName, the payment sheet ensures that the name and postalAddress properties of the contact are populated when it calls this delegate method. This is an implementation of this method:

```
// client_app/merchantapp/ProductCard.m
- (void)
paymentAuthorizationViewController:
    (PKPaymentAuthorizationViewController* _Nonnull)     controller
didSelectShippingContact:
    (PKContact* _Nonnull)                       shipping_contact
completion:
    (void (^ _Nonnull)
        (PKPaymentAuthorizationStatus              status,
         NSArray<PKShippingMethod*>* _Nonnull     shipping_methods,
         NSArray<PKPaymentSummaryItem*>* _Nonnull summary_items)
        )                                         completion
{
    // validate address in shipping_contact parameter.
    // if the address is not valid, set the status argument of
    // the completion block to an appropriate value, such as
    // PKPaymentAuthorizationStatusInvalidShippingPostalAddress.

    completion(
        PKPaymentAuthorizationStatusSuccess,
        _pk_shipping_methods,
        [self computeSummaryItems]
    );
}
```

All this method does is provide a success status, the standard shipping methods, and the computed payment summary items to the payment sheet through the method's completion block. In your app's case, you may need to tailor the returned shipping methods depending on the information contained in the contact argument of the completion block.

User changes shipping method

When the user changes the shipping method, the payment sheet calls the `payment AuthorizationViewController:didSelectShippingMethod:completion:` method of its delegate. Similar to changes in shipping information, you recompute the payment summary items based on the shipping method the user selects. In the `completion` block, provide a success authorization status and the newly computed payment summary items, as shown in this example:

```
// client_app/merchantapp/ProductCard.m
@property PKShippingMethod*   selected_shipping_method;
@property NSString*           shipping_method_name;
...
- (void)
paymentAuthorizationViewController:
    (PKPaymentAuthorizationViewController* _Nonnull)     controller
didSelectShippingMethod:
    (PKShippingMethod* _Nonnull)                shipping_method
completion:
    (void (^ _Nonnull)
        (PKPaymentAuthorizationStatus           status,
         NSArray<PKPaymentSummaryItem*>* _Nonnull summary_items)
        )                                           completion
{
    _selected_shipping_method= shipping_method;
    _shipping_method_name=     shipping_method.identifier;

    completion(
        PKPaymentAuthorizationStatusSuccess,
        [self computeSummaryItems]
    );
}
```

All this method does is store the index of the shipping method chosen, recompute the payment summary item array, and call the completion block with `PKPaymentAuthorizationStatusSuccess` as the `status` argument and the new payment summary items array as the `summary_items` argument.

User authorizes payment request

When the user authorizes the payment request, the payment sheet calls the pa
ymentAuthorizationViewController:didAuthorizePayment:completion:
method in its delegate. In this method, you process the payment (the PKPayment
instance) you get from the payment sheet, a process described in the next chapter.
If the payment is processed successfully, you will call the completion block with
PKPaymentAuthorizationStatusSuccess as the argument. If your validation
checks determine that the payment request contains incorrect information, you can
return values that specify this, such as:

- PKPaymentAuthorizationStatusInvalidBillingPostalAddress
- PKPaymentAuthorizationStatusInvalidShippingPostalAddress
- PKPaymentAuthorizationStatusInvalidShippingContact

Otherwise, for a general failure, including that the issuing bank did not approve the
transaction, you can return PKPaymentAuthorizationStatusFailure.

Here is an with payment sheet:payment request, authorizing" example
implementation of this method:

```
// client_app/merchantapp/ProductCard.m
- (void)
paymentAuthorizationViewController:
    (PKPaymentAuthorizationViewController*)        controller
didAuthorizePayment:
    (PKPayment*)                                   payment_info
completion:
    (void (^)(PKPaymentAuthorizationStatus))       payment_completion
{
    [self process_ApplePay_payment_with_Stripe: payment_info
                            completion: payment_completion
    ];
}
```

Here is an example of the payment sheet:

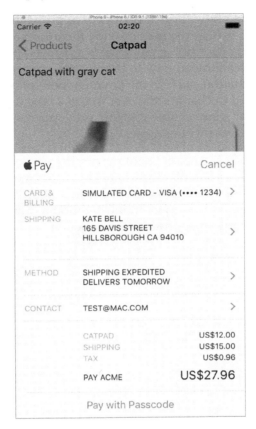

Whether the payment is processed successfully or the user canceled the transaction, it is your responsibility to dismiss the payment sheet when it calls the paymentAuthorizationViewControllerDidFinish: method on its delegate. This is an example of how to do this:

```
// client_app/merchantapp/ProductCard.m
- (void)
paymentAuthorizationViewControllerDidFinish:
    (PKPaymentAuthorizationViewController*)    controller
{
    [self dismissViewControllerAnimated:YES completion:nil];
}
```

In addition to dismissing the payment sheet, you can perform other state-restoring operations as needed.

Summary

In this chapter you learned how the actors in your app's payment authorization workflow work together to help the user provide the information you need to process the payment and order (if the payment is approved by the payment card's issuing bank). The chapter showed how to prepare the payment request with essential payment information, such as the payment networks you support. It described how to respond to changes the user makes to the order in the payment sheet. Finally, the chapter showed how to dismiss the payment sheet after the user authorizes or cancels the payment request.

The next chapter will describe the payment processing workflow, which is where you will process the information obtained here to process the payment through your payment gateway and fulfill the customer's order in your order processing web application. We will consider the payment information required to get the user's payment card's issuing bank to approve the transaction.

4
Payment Processing Workflow

After the user authorizes the payment request, the *user app*, the *payment gateway*, and the *order processing web app* team up to securely deliver payment information to the issuing bank to transfer the funds from the user's account to the acquiring bank and to inform the user of the transaction status (that is, whether it is approved or declined).

The payment processing workflow is made up of three phases:

1. **Preprocess phase**: In this phase, the app gets a charge token from the payment gateway and sends the order information (including the charge token) to the order processing server

2. **Process phase**: In this phase, the order processing web app (running on your server) charges the user's card through the payment gateway, updates the order and inventory data if the charge is successful, and sends the transaction status to the user app

3. **Postprocess phase**: In this, the user app informs the user about the status of the transaction and dismisses the payment sheet

This chapter will do the following:

- Introduce the actors and operations in the payment processing workflow
- Describe each phase of the payment processing workflow and the steps taken within each phase

 As the payment gateway API does not run appropriately in the Simulator app in general, you must use an actual iOS device to test the payment processing workflow in your development environment.

Actors and operations in the processing workflow

The *payment processing workflow* is the process by which the payment information generated by Apple Pay, from the payment request and the information the user entered into the payment sheet, is transmitted to your payment gateway and the card's issuing bank in order to charge the card and make the payment's funds available in your acquiring bank.

The workflow starts when the payment sheet calls the `paymentAuthorizationVi` `ewController:didAuthorizePayment:completion:` delegate method, providing the user app with the general order information (such as the shipping and billing information) and a payment token containing the encrypted payment data.

This diagram depicts the actors, operations, and data that are part of the payment processing workflow:

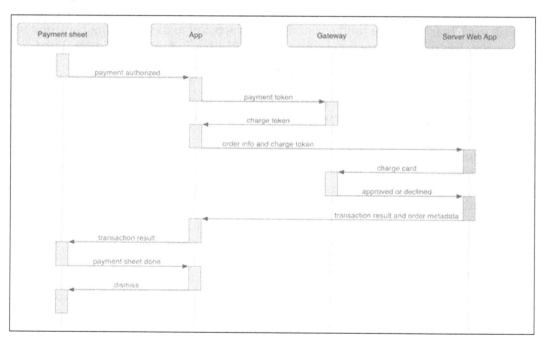

payment_processing_workflow

These are the operations and data that are part of the workflow:

- **payment authorized**: The payment sheet tells the app that the user authorized the payment

- **payment token**: The app provides the payment token to the payment gateway, which returns a **charge token**

- **order info and charge token**: the app sends information about the order and the charge token to the order processing web app

- **charge card**: The web app charges the card through the payment gateway

- **approved or declined**: The payment gateway tells the web app whether the payment is approved or declined

- **transaction result and order metadata**: The web app provides the user app with the result of the transaction and order information such as the order number

- **transaction result**: The app tells the payment sheet the result of the payment transaction—that is, whether it is approved or declined

- **payment sheet done**: The payment sheet tells the app that the transaction is complete

- **dismiss**: The app dismisses the payment sheet

The preprocess phase

In the *Preprocess* phase, the user app uses the payment information that the payment sheet generates (in the form of a PKPayment object) as a result of the user's authorization. The app sends this information to the payment gateway and obtains a charge token (this item may be identified using different names, such as the registration ID, depending on the payment gateway; the order processing web app uses the charge token to charge the user's card). The app then packages the charge token along with pertinent information about the order (such as *billing information, shipping information, shipping method,* and so on) and sends it to the order processing web app on your server.

The following three sections describe the steps of the *Preprocess* phase.

The merchant app receives the payment token

When the user authorizes the payment request, the payment sheet calls the paymen tAuthorizationViewController:didAuthorizePayment:completion: delegate method (which is part of the PKPaymentAuthorizationViewControllerDelegate protocol). This method provides the payment information (a PKPayment object) and a completion block.

These are the components of a `PKPayment` object:

- **payment token** (`PKPaymentToken`): This is generated when the user authorizes the payment request

- **billing contact**: This is the billing contact information, including the e-mail address (`NSString`), name (`NSPersonNameComponents`), phone number (`CNPhoneNumber`), and postal address (`CNPostalAddress`)

- **shipping contact**: This is the shipping contact information (which has the same components as the billing contact)

- **shipping method** (`PKShippingMethod`): This is the shipping method selected by the user

These are the components of a `PKPaymentToken` object:

- **payment data** (an encrypted `NSData` object): This is the data used by the payment gateway and issuing bank to charge the user's card

- **payment method** (`PKPaymentMethod`): This identifies the type of card used for the transaction, such as debit, credit, prepaid, or store card

- **transaction identifier** (`NSString`): This is a user-friendly identifier for the payment transaction

The example merchant app implementation of the `paymentAuthorizationViewController:didAuthorizePayment:completion:` method is listed here:

```
// client_app/merchantapp/ProductCard.m
- (void)
paymentAuthorizationViewController:
    (PKPaymentAuthorizationViewController*)     controller
didAuthorizePayment:
    (PKPayment*)                                payment_info
completion:
    (void (^)(PKPaymentAuthorizationStatus))    payment_completion
{
    [self process_ApplePay_payment_with_Stripe:payment_info
                                completion:payment_completion];
}
```

The method calls `process_ApplePay_payment_with_Stripe:completion:` to start processing the payment. This method is tailored for a particular payment gateway. The `payment_info` parameter contains the payment token, and the shipping and billing information requested in the payment request. The `payment_completion` parameter defines the block that tells the payment sheet that the transaction is processed.

The merchant app receives the charge token from the payment gateway

After the app gets the payment information (a PKPayment object), it uses the payment gateway API to obtain a charge token, which is used by the order processing web app to charge the card. (Some payment gateways provide a native iOS API to issue the charge token; others require that the app makes an HTTP request to their payment server.) The APIs of some payment gateways operate on the payment token (PKPaymentToken), while others require the PKPayment object.

In the example merchant app, the process_ApplePay_payment_with_Stripe:completion: method of the ProductCard class calls the native iOS API provided by the Stripe payment gateway, which operates on the PKPayment object, returning a charge token (an STPToken object). Other payment gateways have a similar native or web API that provides the same functionality.

This is the process_ApplePay_payment_with_Stripe:completion: method in the example merchant app:

```objc
// client_app/merchantapp/ProductCard.m
- (void)
process_ApplePay_payment_with_Stripe:
   (PKPayment*)                               payment_info
completion:
   (void (^)(PKPaymentAuthorizationStatus))   payment_completion
{
   [[STPAPIClient sharedClient]
      createTokenWithPayment: payment_info
               completion: ^
   (STPToken* charge_token, NSError* error)
   {
      if (error)
      {
         NSLog(@"error creating STPToken object");
         payment_completion(PKPaymentAuthorizationStatusFailure);
      }
      else
         [self backend_process_payment_info: payment_info
                              gateway: @"stripe"
                         charge_token: charge_token
                           completion: payment_completion];
   }];
}
```

If the method that creates the charge token (createTokenWithPayment:complet
ion: of the STPAPIClient class) reports an error, this method calls the payment
completion block with the PKPaymentAuthorizationStatusFailure argument,
which effectively ends the transaction. Otherwise, it calls the backend_process_
payment_info:gateway:charge_token:completion: method, which is described
in the next section.

The merchant app sends the order information to the order processing system

After obtaining the payment information (PKPayment) from the payment sheet and
the charge token from the payment gateway, the app packages the charge token and
other information required by the order processing web app and sends it to your
server through an HTTP request.

In the example merchant app, the backend_process_payment_
info:gateway:charge_token:completion: method of the ProductCard class
packages the required information into a JSON object (the payload) and sends it to the
order processing web app through an HTTP POST request to the http://red:12345/
payment unique resource identifier (URI). Take a look at the following code:

```
// client_app/merchantapp/ProductCard.m
- (void)
backend_process_payment_info:
    (PKPayment*)                              payment_info
gateway:
    (NSString*)                           gateway
charge_token:
    (id)                                  charge_token
completion:
    (void (^)(PKPaymentAuthorizationStatus))  payment_completion
{
    RestIO* rest_io= [RestIO sharedRestIO];
    {
        AppDelegate* app_delegate=
            [UIApplication sharedApplication].delegate;
        NSString* payment_charge_uri=
            [NSString stringWithFormat:@"%@%@",
                app_delegate.rest_io_host,
                @"/payment"];

        NSNumber* total_in_cents= (NSNumber*)
```

```objc
[_payment_request
    .paymentSummaryItems
        [_payment_request.paymentSummaryItems.count - 1]
    .amount
    decimalNumberByMultiplyingBy:
        [NSDecimalNumber decimalNumberWithString: @"100"]
];
NSString* currency= _payment_request.currencyCode;

NSString* contact_name=
    [payment_info.shippingContact.name.givenName
        stringByAppendingString:
            [@" " stringByAppendingString:
                payment_info.shippingContact.name.familyName]];

// collect info required by order processing webapp
NSDictionary* order_info_package_dictionary= @
{
    @"gateway"       : gateway,
    @"source"        : ((STPToken*)charge_token).tokenId,
    @"amount"        : total_in_cents,
    @"currency"      : currency,
    @"description"   :
        _payment_request.paymentSummaryItems[0].label,
    @"shipping_contact"     : contact_name,
    @"shipping_email"       :
        payment_info.shippingContact.emailAddress,
    @"shipping_street"      :
        payment_info.shippingContact.postalAddress.street,
    @"shipping_city"        :
        payment_info.shippingContact.postalAddress.city,
    @"shipping_state"       :
        payment_info.shippingContact.postalAddress.state,
    @"shipping_zip"         :
        payment_info.shippingContact.postalAddress.postalCode,
    @"shipping_method_name" :
        payment_info.shippingMethod.identifier
};

NSData* order_info_package_json;
{
    NSError* error;
```

```objc
    order_info_package_json=
       [NSJSONSerialization
          dataWithJSONObject: order_info_package_dictionary
                    options: NSJSONWritingPrettyPrinted
                      error: &error];
    NSAssert(!error, @"error converting %@ to JSON", error);
  }


  // send order information to order processing web app
  [rest_io postResourceAtURI: payment_charge_uri
                       body: order_info_package_json
                 completion: ^
(NSURLResponse* response, NSData* data)
  {
     if (((NSHTTPURLResponse*)response).statusCode == 200)
     {
        NSDictionary* result;
        {
           NSError* error;
           result=
              [NSJSONSerialization
                 JSONObjectWithData: data
                            options: 0
                              error: &error];
           if (error)
              [NSException
                 raise: @"JSONDeserializationException"
                format: @"error deserializing JSON"];
        }
        NSString* status= (NSString*)result[@"status"];
        payment_completion(
           [status isEqual: @"succeeded"]?
              PKPaymentAuthorizationStatusSuccess :
              PKPaymentAuthorizationStatusFailure
        );
     }
     else
        payment_completion(
           PKPaymentAuthorizationStatusFailure);
  }];
  }
}
```

The `payment_info` parameter is the `PKPayment` object provided by the payment sheet in the `paymentAuthorizationViewController:didAuthorizePayment:completion:` delegate method. The `gateway` parameter identifies the payment gateway the app uses to get the charge token; this could be useful for merchant apps that use more than one payment gateway but only one order processing web app. The `charge_token` parameter is the charge token obtained from the payment gateway API. The `payment_completion` parameter is the same completion block provided in the `paymentAuthorizationViewController:didAuthorizePayment:completion:` delegate method.

In the order processing web app, the handler for the `/payment` request takes a JSON object (which is stored in the `order_info_package_json` variable in the `backend_process_payment_info:` method) with the required information. In the example project's web app, this information is the name of the payment gateway, the information the payment processor requires to charge the payment card (the payment token, the payment amount, and the payment's currency), and the shipping details.

The process phase

In the *Process* phase of the payment processing workflow, the order processing web app charges the user's card, updates the ordering and inventory data, and returns the transaction's status (that is, whether it is approved or declined) to the user app on the user's device as an HTTP response to the app's original HTTP request. This web app uses the payment gateway's server-side API to communicate with it.

In the example order processing web app (a Node.js web app), the HTTP request from the user app is handled by the middleware, as follows:

```
// server_app/red.js
// payment middleware
server.post('/payment', function(request, response, next)
{
  // 1. parse request
  var order_info_package= JSON.parse(request.body);

  // process charge token
  if (order_info_package.gateway == 'stripe')
  {
    // 2. charge payment card
    var charge= stripe.charges.create
    (
      {
        amount       : order_info_package.amount,
```

```
    currency    : order_info_package.currency,
    source      : order_info_package.source,
    description :
        'charge for ' + order_info_package.description
},
function(error, charge)
{
    var transaction_info=
    {
        id     : charge.id,
        status : charge.status
    }

    if (error)
        console.log('there's an error creating a charge: '
            + error);
    else
    {
        // 3.a update inventory
        // ...

        // 3.b create order
        var order= models.Order(
        {
            date                : new Date(),
            description         :
                order_info_package.description,
            shipping_email      :
                order_info_package.shipping_email,
            shipping_street     :
                order_info_package.shipping_street,
            shipping_city       :
                order_info_package.shipping_city,
            shipping_state      :
                order_info_package.shipping_state,
            shipping_zip        :
                order_info_package.shipping_zip,
            shipping_method_name :
                order_info_package.shipping_method_name,
            total_price         :
```

```
                    order_info_package.amount,
                stripe_charge_id      : charge.id
            });
            order.save();

            transaction_info.order_id= order._id;
        }

        // 4. send transaction result to customer's device
        response.send(transaction_info);
        }
    );
    }
    next();
});
```

This middleware is divided into four steps:

1. Parse the request's JSON content.

2. Charge the card using the API provided by the payment gateway; in this case, the `charge` function is provided in the `Stripe JavaScript` module.

3. If the transaction is approved, create the order and update the quantity on hand of the ordered product.

4. Send the transaction result (including the order number if the payment was approved) to the user's device.

The postprocess phase

In the *Postprocess* phase of the payment processing workflow, the app analyzes the response the order processing web app gave to the HTTP request that the app made in the *Preprocess* phase. In general terms, the response indicates whether the issuing bank approved or declined the payment. The response may also include an order number, order status, and other details that you deem useful for the user; the app may display a custom confirmation sheet containing this information. Finally, the app dismisses the payment sheet.

The following three sections describe the steps of the *Postprocess* phase.

The merchant app receives the transaction status from the order processing web app

The example user app receives the response from the order processing web app in a block in the `backend_process_payment_info:gateway:charge_token:completion:` method. The block's arguments are an `NSURLResponse` object and an `NSData` object. The code that processes the response and returned data is highlighted here:

```
// client_app/merchantapp/ProductCard.m
- (void)
backend_process_payment_info:
    (PKPayment*)                            payment_info
gateway:
    (NSString*)                             gateway
charge_token:
    (id)                                    charge_token
completion:
    (void (^)(PKPaymentAuthorizationStatus))    payment_completion
{
    RestIO* rest_io= [RestIO sharedRestIO];
    {
        ...
        // send order information to order processing web app
        [rest_io postResourceAtURI: payment_charge_uri
                        body: order_info_package_json
                    completion: ^
        (NSURLResponse* response, NSData* data)
        {
            if (((NSHTTPURLResponse*)response).statusCode == 200)
            {
                NSDictionary* result;
                {
                    NSError* error;
                    result=
                        [NSJSONSerialization
                            JSONObjectWithData: data
                                    options: 0
                                        error: &error];
                    if (error)
                        [NSException
                            raise: @"JSONDeserializationException"
                            format: @"error deserializing JSON"];
                }
```

```
        NSString* status= (NSString*)result[@"status"];
        payment_completion(
            [status isEqual: @"succeeded"]?
                PKPaymentAuthorizationStatusSuccess :
                PKPaymentAuthorizationStatusFailure
        );
    }
    else
        payment_completion(
            PKPaymentAuthorizationStatusFailure);
    }];
    }
}
```

If the HTTP response code is `200`, there were no server-side problems generating the response. In this case, the method transforms the JSON that makes up the returned content into an `NSDictionary` object (`result`), which contains several entries describing the transaction (refer to the *Process* Phase section for details). The method focuses on one entry in particular: the `"status"` key.

The merchant app conveys the transaction status to the user

After the example merchant app receives the response from the order processing web app (as a JSON object in the HTTP response payload), it determines whether the transaction was approved or declined by examining the returned data. Then, it calls the `payment_completion` block to inform the payment sheet of the transaction status so that the sheet can convey this information to the user. The highlighted code in this listing performs this process:

```
// client_app/merchantapp/ProductCard.m
- (void)
backend_process_payment_info:
    (PKPayment*)                                    payment_info
gateway:
    (NSString*)                                     gateway
charge_token:
    (id)                                            charge_token
completion:
    (void (^)(PKPaymentAuthorizationStatus))        payment_completion
{
    RestIO* rest_io= [RestIO sharedRestIO];
```

```
{
    ...
    // send order information to order processing web app
    [rest_io postResourceAtURI: payment_charge_uri
                        body: order_info_package_json
                  completion: ^
    (NSURLResponse* response, NSData* data)
    {
        if (((NSHTTPURLResponse*)response).statusCode == 200)
        {
            NSDictionary* result;
            {
                NSError* error;
                result=
                    [NSJSONSerialization
                        JSONObjectWithData: data
                                   options: 0
                                     error: &error];
                if (error)
                    [NSException
                         raise: @"JSONDeserializationException"
                        format: @"error deserializing JSON"];
            }
            NSString* status= (NSString*)result[@"status"];
            payment_completion(
                [status isEqual: @"succeeded"]?
                    PKPaymentAuthorizationStatusSuccess :
                    PKPaymentAuthorizationStatusFailure
            );
        }
        else
            payment_completion(
                PKPaymentAuthorizationStatusFailure);
    }];
    }
}
```

If the value for the "status" key in the returned data is "succeeded", it means that the payment was approved by the issuing bank, and the funds will be available in the acquiring bank sometime in the near future. In this case, the method calls the completion block the payment sheet provided (payment_completion) to indicate that the payment was approved with PKPaymentAuthorizationStatusSuccess as the argument. If the HTTP response code is not 200 or the value for the "status" key in the returned data is not "succeeded", the method calls the completion block with PKPaymentAuthorizationStatusFailure as the argument.

Calling the `payment_completion` block with `PKPaymentAuthorizationStatusSuccess` results in the payment sheet displaying a checkmark, indicating that the payment was approved, as shown in the following screenshot:

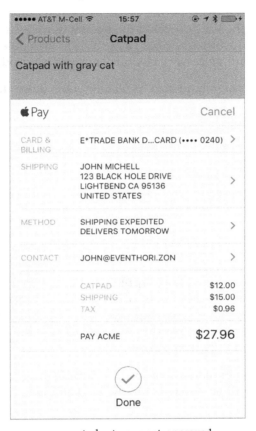

payment_sheet-payment_approved

You can display an additional sheet providing more information about the transaction, such as the order number and estimated delivery date.

The merchant app dismisses the payment sheet

When the payment sheet is done (either because the transaction was approved or declined, or because the user canceled the transaction), it calls the paymentAuthorizationViewControllerDidFinish: delegate method. Here, you can perform any necessary cleanup or app-state updates.

This is how the example merchant app implements the delegate method:

```
// client_app/merchantapp/ProductCard.m
- (void) paymentAuthorizationViewControllerDidFinish:
            (PKPaymentAuthorizationViewController*)
                                        controller
{
    [self dismissViewControllerAnimated:YES completion:nil];
}
```

Summary

In this chapter, you have learned how Apple Pay payments are processed. The chapter has described each of the phases of the payment processing workflow, identifying the steps that make up each phase. The *Processing phase*, in particular, is where all the components are linked to securely charge the user's card and make the funds available in your acquiring bank.

The chapter has based its explanations on the example project that accompanies this book. This project will be described in the next chapter.

5
Designing an Order Management Server

If you have a business that provides physical goods to your customers, it is important that you have a reliable order management server. Depending on your customers' needs, you may need to provide access to the server from client apps running on web browsers, web servers, or mobile devices. This book focuses on client apps running on iPhone and iPad devices, and in the Simulator app.

Generally, a client-/server-based order capture and order processing system has these components:

- **Server**: This runs the order processing web app, database management system, and other server-side processes. The web app implements HTTP-based API clients that are used to request and submit information. Through this API, the web app provides product information to clients, and processes payment and order information submitted by clients.

- **Client**: This runs the client app. The client app calls the API that the order processing web app provides to request and submit information to the web app.

For the purposes of this book, an *order management web app* is a process that responds to HTTP requests. In this book's example project, this process provides inventory and shipping method information to clients and processes the payment information clients submitted to it (which includes information about the item ordered, shipping details, and so on).

Client apps interact with the server through HTTP requests. In your development environment, the order management web app runs on your development computer, and the client app runs in a simulator or an iOS device that supports Apple Pay.

This chapter describes the following:

- The main characteristics of an order management server
- Its database structure and client API

Configuring an order management server web app

A *web server* is a computer that stores information, modifies it, and provides clients with access to it. These clients can request information or ask the server to process data in a specific way, which can result in a change to the data stored on the server and the client receiving a representation of this data. Practically, any computer can be a web server. A web app is a process that runs on a web server and serves content to clients through HTTP requests. In production environments, web apps run on specially configured web servers, which provide redundancy, replication, and other features to ensure robustness, high performance, and safety, among other characteristics. However, you do not need a fully fledged web server to run a web app. You can run a web app on your development computer.

An *order management server* is a web app that runs on a computer that is accessible to clients. In your development environment (which is comprised of your computer, developer toolset, and iOS devices), the server web app runs on your computer, and the client app runs in a simulator on your computer or an iOS device.

 The hardware and software configurations of the server and clients are numerous. This chapter describes a configuration for development on a single Mac using the Simulator app and an iOS device that can send HTTP requests to this computer. This configuration is not suitable for testing or deployment. Consult a deployment engineer when you are ready to test or deploy your apps in more realistic configurations.

To exercise all the components of a client app that supports Apple Pay (such as this book's example app, the Merchant app), you must run the client app on an iOS device. In general, client-side payment gateway software does not operate effectively in simulators.

A client app can access the server web app directly (that is, if both processes are running on the same computer, such as when the client runs in iOS Simulator), through an internal network with the client running on an iOS device (within a subnet), or through the Internet using a web server that is accessible through the public Internet (either for wide-scale testing or production). The example project uses Node.js to implement the server web app. Node.js is an environment used to develop server-side apps.

Defining order management data structures

An order management system has, as a minimum, data structures representing products available for sale (inventory) and orders. To support the Apple Pay workflow, the system should also have a structure representing the supported shipping methods. The example project uses a MongoDB database to store this data, and the Mongoose data modeling module for Node.js. MongoDB is a document-based database system. Mongoose makes it easier to create documents from schemas and access the data in these documents.

The database for the example order management system has three collections: Product, ShippingMethod, and Order. A collection is similar to a table in a relational database system.

The Product collection stores information about each product offered for sale. The following table shows the fields available for product records within the collection:

Field name	Description
name	This is the name of the product
description	This is a phrase describing the product
image_uri	This is a URI identifying an image of the product
quantity_on_hand	This is the number of units of the product in stock
price	This is the sale price of each unit of the product

The `ShippingMethod` collection stores information about the shipping methods available. The following table shows the fields for shipping records:

Field name	Description
name	This is the name of the shipping method
description	This is a phrase stating the shipment duration in days
transit_days	This is a number stating the shipment duration in days
price	This is the price for the shipping method

The `Order` collection stores information about each order processed by the order management system. These are the fields for order records:

Field name	Description
date	This is the date-time group that the order was processed in
description	This is the name of the product sold (one product per order)
shipping_contact	This is the name of the person identified as the shipping contact
shipping_email	This is the e-mail address of the shipping contact
shipping_street	This is the street of the shipping address
shipping_city	This is the city of the shipping address
shipping_state	This is the state of the shipping address
shipping_zip	This is the zip code of the shipping address
shipping_method_name	This is the name of the shipping method used for the order

This is the Node.js code that defines the structure of the three collections:

```
var mongoose= require('mongoose');
var Schema=   mongoose.Schema;

var Product_schema= new Schema({
    name:             String,
    description:      String,
    image_uri:        String,
    quantity_on_hand: Number,
```

```
    price:           String
});

var ShippingMethod_schema= new Schema({
    name:          String,
    description:   String,
    transit_days:  Number,
    price:         String
});

var Order_schema= new Schema({
    date                  : String,
    description           : String,
    shipping_contact      : String,
    shipping_email        : String,
    shipping_street       : String,
    shipping_city         : String,
    shipping_state        : String,
    shipping_zip          : String,
    shipping_method_name  : String,
    total_price           : String,
    stripe_charge_id      : String
});

exports.Product=
    mongoose.model('Product',          Product_schema);
exports.ShippingMethod=
    mongoose.model('ShippingMethod', ShippingMethod_schema);
exports.Order=
    mongoose.model('Order',            Order_schema);
```

Providing inventory information to clients

The order management system implements three REST APIs (known as middleware in Node.js parlance) to provide inventory and shipping method information to clients. These are as follows:

- /shipping_methods: This returns the list of supported shipping methods
- /inventory: This returns the product catalog
- /product_image/<image_name>: This returns the image used to represent a product to the user

When the client app is launched, it requests the list of shipping methods supported by the system (the `application:didFinishLaunchingWithOptions:` method in `AppDelegate.m`). Before displaying the list of the available products in the product list screen, the app requests the product catalog (the `viewDidLoad` method in `ProductList.m`). When the app is about to display the card for a particular product (after the user selects a product in the product list screen), it requests the product's image from the server (the `viewDidLoad` method in `ProductCard.m`).

> For development, the URIs used by the example app (Merchant app) specify a process name (but not a real web address) and port number to access the order management server web app (for example, `http://red:12345/inventory`). When you deploy your app to a production environment (that is, the real world), you must use a real, appropriately configured web server to run your web app, and URIs that point to a public web address, such as `http://red.com/inventory`.

This is the Node.js code that implements the middleware introduced earlier in this section:

```
// server_app/red.js

// load required modules
var models=      require('./lib/inventory_models.js');
var assert=      require('assert');
var mongoose=    require('mongoose');
var restify=     require('restify');
var stripe=      require('stripe')('<my_key>')
var server=      restify.createServer();
server.use(restify.bodyParser());

// specify the data models
Product=         models.Product;
ShippingMethod=  models.ShippingMethod;
Order=           models.Order;

// connect to the red MongoDB database
mongoose.connect('mongodb://localhost/red');

protocol=   'http://';
hostname=   'red';
port=       12345;
base_uri=   protocol + hostname + ':' + port;
```

```
console.log(base_uri);

// initialize Product collection, if needed
Product.find(function(error, _products)
{
    if (_products.length == 0)
    {
        console.log('initializing product collection');
        models.Product(
        {
            name:             'Clock',
            description:       'Wooden clock',
            quantity_on_hand: 10,
            price:            '50.00',
            image_uri:        base_uri + '/product_image/clock.jpeg'
        }).save();
        ...
    }
});

// load Product collection into products
var products= new Array();
Product.find(function(error, _products)
{
    products= _products;
});

// initialize ShippingMethods collection, if needed
ShippingMethod.find(function(error, _shipping_methods)
{
    if (_shipping_methods.length == 0)
    {
        console.log('initializing shipping-method collection');
        models.ShippingMethod({
            name:        'Free',
            description: 'Delivers in seven days',
            transit_days: 7,
            price:       '0.00'
        }).save();
        ...
    }
})

// load ShippingMethod collection into shipping_methods
var shipping_methods= new Array();
ShippingMethod.find(function(error, _shipping_methods)
```

```
{
    shipping_methods= _shipping_methods;
});

// ** start middleware (client API) **
//    /product_image/<name> API:
//       provides product image from
//       <project_dir>/public/product_image/<name>
server.get(/\/product_image\/?.*/,
    restify.serveStatic( { directory: '../public' }));

//    /inventory API:
//       provides current inventory from Product document
server.get('/inventory', function(request, response, next)
{
    response.send(products);
    next();
});

//    /shippng_methods API:
//       provides shipping methods from ShippingMethod document
server.get('/shipping_methods', function(request, response, next)
{
    response.send(shipping_methods);
    next();
});
...
// ** end middleware (client API) **

// listen for HTTP requests
server.listen(12345);
```

Processing orders from clients

The example order management system server web app processes orders in a single function, payment (described in *Chapter 4, Payment Processing Workflow*), which clients execute through an HTTP POST request to the http://red:12345/payment URI.

First, the function attempts to charge the customer card. If the charge is successful, the function adds a record to the Order collection using the order information that the client provided. When done, the function returns information about the payment transaction and the new order (if it was created) to the client.

Refer to the *Process Phase* section in *Chapter 4, Payment Processing Workflow*, for details about the implementation of the payment function.

Implementing secure communication

The configuration described in the preceding sections is only for development. There are several things you need to do when deploying an order management system web app for use by real customers. The client apps used by your customers must also be secure.

Firstly, instead of using a process name and port number in URIs, client apps should use URIs based on a web address, such as `http://red.com`. You should also configure a computer as your publicly accessible web server, which runs your server process. Depending on the expected traffic volume, you may configure your web server to run several instances of the server web app to process requests from several clients concurrently.

Secondly, you must ensure that the data transmitted between the server and client is secure. By securing data transmission, you ensure that only authorized entities receive the data, that the data is not modified in transit, and that the data cannot be read by third parties. One way to do this is to use the **HTTPS (HTTP Secure)** protocol instead of HTTP to transmit messages and data between server and client.

You can learn about adding HTTPS support to client apps in Apple's Developer Library. For information about implementing HTTPS in your web server, consult the appropriate documentation.

Summary

This chapter has described the design and implementation of a simple web app to serve as an order management system that provides inventory data to client apps and processes orders submitted from the client apps running in the iOS Simulator app, and on iPhone or iPad devices, which support Apple Pay. The chapter has also mentioned the critical security measures you need to implement in web servers and client apps to ensure secure communication between them. The next chapter will provide essential information about the main Apple Pay API used by client apps.

6
Apple Pay API Summary

You process Apple Pay transactions in three phases:

1. **Preparation**: Create a payment request and populate it with payment information and details about the product the user is purchasing.

2. **Payment sheet interaction**: Respond to user interactions with the payment sheet (such as changes to the shipping address or the desired shipping method) through the methods of the `PKPaymentAuthorizationViewControllerDelegate` protocol.

3. **Payment processing**: Process the Apple Pay transaction on the user's device and your own servers through the API provided by your payment gateway and HTTP requests to your order processing web app.

Earlier chapters showed the workflows you use to interact with the major actors in Apple Pay transactions. This chapter provides helpful information on the classes, methods, and properties of the Apple Pay API that you must become familiar with to use it effectively. However, when you need even more detailed information, you should consult the Apple developer documentation.

In this chapter, you will learn about the major Apple Pay classes involved in payment transactions, such as the `PKPaymentReqest` and `PKPaymentSummaryItem` classes. You will also learn how to respond to payment sheet events through the `PKPaymentAuthorizationViewControllerDelegate` protocol. Finally, the chapter will describe the additional classes that the Apple Pay API uses to work with addresses, such as the `PKContact` class.

This chapter covers the following topics:

- Major Apple Pay classes involved in payment transactions, such as the `PKPaymentReqest` and `PKPaymentSummaryItem` classes

- Responses to payment sheet events through the `PKPaymentAuthorizationViewControllerDelegate` protocol

- Additional classes that the Apple Pay API uses to work

Main classes

This section describes the major Apple Pay classes you use to process Apple Pay transactions. These classes include:

- `PKPaymentButton`: You use this class to display a **Pay** button, which the user uses to begin an Apple Pay transaction.

- `PKPaymentRequest`: This class represents a payment request, which the user authorizes or cancels in the payment sheet.

- `PKPaymentSummaryItem`: Instances of this class represent summary items (such as subtotal, shipping costs, and total) in the payment sheet.

- `PKPaymentMethod`: This class provides access to information about the payment card used in Apple Pay transaction.

- `PKShippingMethod`: Instances of this class represent the shipment methods you support.

- `PKPaymentAuthorizationViewController`: This class determines whether the user can use Apple Pay on the device. It is also used to present the payment sheet on the screen.

- `PKPayment`: Instances of this class store payment information for Apple Pay transactions.

- `PKPaymentToken`: Instances of this class contain encrypted payment information ready to be submitted to a payment processor to charge the user's payment card.

The PKPaymentButton class

The `PKPaymentButton` class provides users with a button they tap to start an Apple Pay transaction. You should use Apple Pay buttons to start only Apple Pay transactions.

Before displaying the **Apple Pay** button, you must ensure that the device supports Apple Pay by calling the canMakePayments method of the PKPaymentAuthorizationViewController class. You should also call either canMakePaymentsUsingNetworks: or canMakePaymentsUsingNetworks:capabilities: of the same class to ensure that the user's payment cards support the payment networks and payment processor capabilities you require. Refer to *The PKPaymentAuthorizationViewController class* later in this section for details.

If the device does not support Apple Pay, or the payment cards that the user has added to the device are not compatible with the payment networks and payment processor capabilities you require, use a standard button with a title such as **Buy** to start standard payment transactions.

Creating the button

Use this method to create a **Apple Pay** button. Use Apple Pay buttons only for Apple Pay transactions.

+buttonWithType:style

This method provides an **Apple Pay** button.

Here are the arguments:

- type (PKPaymentButtonType): This specifies the button's title. The options are plain (**Pay**), buy (**Buy with Pay**), and set up (**Set up Pay**). To learn more about using the last option, refer to *Apple Pay Programming Guide* in the Apple Developer library.

- style (PKPaymentButtonStyle): This specifies the button's appearance. Use it to ensure that the button stands out from the background. The options are white, white outline, and black.

The PKPaymentRequest class

The PKPaymentRequest class represents a request for payment for particular goods. This is the main class you use in Apple Pay transactions. You can use one instance of this class per Apple Pay transaction. A payment request contains information about the merchant requesting the payment, the country where the payment is to be processed, the currency to use, the price of the items for which the payment is requested (including shipping cost, tax, and so on), and the supported payment networks (such as Amex, Discover, and Visa).

When the user authorizes a payment request in the payment sheet, you will get a PKPayment object, which you need to submit to your payment gateway to obtain a PKPaymentToken object (or a substitute), which, in turn, you can use in your order processing system to charge the user's payment card.

Payment processing information

These required properties specify information that your payment gateway uses to process the payment. These should be the first things you set on a payment request.

countryCode (NSString*)

This is a two-letter code (ISO 3166) for the country in which the payment is to be processed, for example "US".

This code sets the countryCode property of a payment request to US, as follows:

```
_payment_request.countryCode=@"US";
```

currencyCode (NSString*)

This is a three-letter code (ISO 4217) for the currency to be used to process the payment, for example "USD".

merchantCapabilities (PKMerchantCapability)

These are the payment processing protocols your payment gateway supports. The 3-D Secure protocol is required. Other protocols available are EMV (Europay, MasterCard, Visa), credit card, and debit card.

These constants identify the following payment processing capabilities that Apple Pay supports:

- PKMerchantCapability3DS
- PKMerchantCapabilityEMV
- PKMerchantCapabilityCredit
- PKMerchantCapabilityDebit

The following code sets the merchantCapabilities property of a payment request to 3D Secure and EMV:

```
_payment_request.merchantCapabilities=
   PKMerchantCapability3DS | PKMerchantCapabilityEMV;
```

merchantIdentifier (NSString*)

This is a merchant identifier stored in your project's `Entitlements` file.

supportedNetworks (NSArray<NSString*>*)

This includes the payment networks (or associations) you support. The options available are Discover, MasterCard, Visa, and private label (store card).

These constants identify the following payment networks that Apple Pay supports:

- `PKPaymentNetworkAmex`
- `PKPaymentNetworkDiscover`
- `PKPaymentNetworkMasterCard`
- `PKPaymentNetworkPrivateLabel`
- `PKPaymentNetworkVisa`

For example, this code sets the `supportedNetworks` property of a payment request to Amex and MasterCard:

```
_payment_request.supportedNetworks=
    PKPaymentNetworkAmex | PKPaymentNetworkMasterCard;
```

Payment summary items

Summary items identify and price the product that the customer is purchasing (the subtotal) and related items, such as the tax, shipping cost, and total.

paymentSummaryItems (NSArray<PKPaymentSummaryItem*>*)

This is an array of summary items, which specify a label and price for each item. Additionally, you can identify an item as *pending* (the price is not yet set, but it will be determined after the service is complete, such as for a taxi ride) or *final*. Refer to the *The PKSummaryItem class* section for details.

The required address fields

These properties specify which fields of the billing and shipping address you require to be entered in the payment sheet so that they are available in the `PKPayment` object provided by the payment sheet when the user authorizes the payment request.

requiredBillingAddressFields (PKAddressField), requiredShippingAddressFields (PKAddressField)

If you require a name, e-mail, and postal address in the shipping information, you can use code similar to this:

```
payment_request.requiredShippingAddressFields=
    PKAddressFieldName | PKAddressFieldEmail |
PKAddressFieldPostalAddress;
```

These are the address field specifier constants:

- `PKAddressFieldNone` (no field is required)
- `PKAddressFieldPostalAddress`
- `PKAddressFieldPhone`
- `PKAddressFieldEmail`
- `PKAddressFieldName`
- `PKAddressFieldAll`

Billing and shipping contacts

These properties specify the billing and shipping contact information. You can set them before displaying the payment sheet (however, this is not recommended because the user is most likely to have up-to-date contact information). The user can also change them by picking or specifying a different contact on the payment sheet.

billingContact (PKContact*), shippingContact (PKContact*)

These are the components of a `PKContact` object:

- `emailAddress`   `(NSString*)`
- `name`   `(NSPersonNameComponents*)`
- `phoneNumber`   `(CNPhoneNumber*)`
- `postalAddress`   `(CNPostalAddress*)`

Shipping methods

Shipping methods are the shipping options (carriers or speed) that you support.

shippingMethods (NSArray<PKShippingMethod*>*)

This property contains the set of shipping methods available to the customer.

Each `PKShippingMethod` object has these properties:

- `detail` (`NSString*`): This describes the shipping method to the user, for example "Delivers in four days".

- `identifier` (`NSString*`): This identifies the shipping method within the app. When the user selects a shipping method, use this property to identify the method chosen.

Shipping type

This specifies the way in which the product is transported, for example whether it is shipped by the merchant, or picked up by the customer from the merchant's store.

shippingType (PKShippingType)

These are the shipping types available:

- `PKShippingTypeShipping` (default): The merchant ships the product to the customer using the shipping method that the customer selects.

- `PKShippingTypeDelivery`: The merchant delivers (using a vehicle) the product to the customer. This is used for food, groceries, furniture, or specialty items that cannot be shipped.

- `PKShippingTypeStorePickup`: The customer picks up the product from the merchant's store. In this case, set `shippingContact` to your store's address or hide it from the payment sheet by setting `requiredShippingAddressFields` to `PKAddressFieldNone`. Remember to confirm the pickup location with the customer in a reliable way.

- `PKShippingTypeServicePickup`: The merchant picks up an object from the address specified in `shippingContact` (for example, when the customer is paying to have something delivered).

Application data

This property stores the hash of an NSData object.

applicationData (NSData*)

When set, this property contains a hash of the data specified (it does not, however, contain the value of the data). If your payment gateway supports it, the paymentData property of the PKPaymentToken object you get from the payment gateway API is set to the same hash value generated when you set applicationData. You can send this hash as part of sending payment information to your order-processing server. Separately, you can send the actual data to your server. You can then compute the hash on your server and compare the two hashes to ensure that the data was not changed in transit.

The PKPaymentSummaryItem class

The PKPaymentSummaryItem class represents an item for which the customer is paying, such as the subtotal representing the product price, tax, shipping cost, and so on. You can identify one or more items as "pending" (the price cannot be determined until some time in the future) or "final". The payment sheet does not show the price of "pending" items; therefore, you should set the price of such items to zero. You can compute the actual price when the service (such as a taxi ride) is completed and report it to the customer when the transaction is complete.

Creating a summary item

These methods create summary items.

+summaryItemWithLabel:amount:

This creates a "final" summary item with a label and amount.

+summaryItemWithLabel:amount:type:

This creates a "pending" or "final" summary item with a label and amount.

The following code creates a "pending" summary item:

```
PKPaymentSummaryItem* trip=
    [PKPaymentSummaryItem summaryItemWithLabel: @"Trip"
                                        amount: [NSDecimalNumber zero]
                                          type:
PKPaymentSummaryItemTypePending] ;
```

Summary item components

These properties access the components of a summary item.

label (NSString*)

This is the label of the summary item.

amount (NSDecimalNumber*)

This is the price of the summary item (it is shown in the payment sheet if the item is "final").

Pending or final

This property determines the type of the summary item.

type (PKPaymentSummaryItemType)

This specifies whether the item is "pending" or "final."

These are the possible values of the `type` property:

- `PKPaymentSummaryItemTypeFinal`
- `PKPaymentSummaryItemTypePending`

The PKPaymentMethod class

The `PKPaymentMethod` class provides access to information about the payment card used in an Apple Pay transaction. When the user selects a payment card in the payment sheet, the payment sheet calls the `paymentAuthorizationView Controller:didSelectPaymentMethod:completion:` method of its delegate.

Card tame

This property identifies the payment card for the `payment` method.

displayName (NSString*)

This identifies the payment card to the user.

Card type

This property identifies the type of the payment card.

type (PKPaymentMethodType)

This identifies the type of payment card used (Amex, Visa, and so on). Old cards may not have this information; in this case, the value of this property is `PKPaymentMethodTypeUnknown`.

These constants identify the types of cards that Apple Pay supports:

*   `PKPaymentMethodTypeUnknown`
*   `PKPaymentMethodTypeDebit`
*   `PKPaymentMethodTypeCredit`
*   `PKPaymentMethodTypePrepaid`
*   `PKPaymentMethodTypeStore`

Payment network

This property identifies the payment network.

network (NSString*)

This identifies the card's payment network (or association).

These constants identify the payment networks that Apple Pay supports:

*   `PKPaymentNetworkAmex`
*   `PKPaymentNetworkDiscover`
*   `PKPaymentNetworkMasterCard`
*   `PKPaymentNetworkPrivateLabel` (this is for store cards)
*   `PKPaymentNetworkVisa`

Payment pass

This property is used with a payment pass.

paymentPass (PKPaymentPass*)

You can use this, for example, to support custom branded payment cards. Take a look at Apple's documentation for more details.

The PKShippingMethod class

The PKShippingMethod class represents a shipping method you support for the delivery of goods to a customer.

User-friendly description

This property provides the user with information about the shipping method.

detail (NSString*)

This describes the shipping method to the user, for example: *"Delivers in four days"*.

App-level identifier

This property identifies the shipping method within the app.

identifier (NSString*)

When the user changes the shipping method, use this property to identify the shipping method chosen.

The PKPaymentAuthorizationViewController class

The PKPaymentAuthorizationViewController class has two functions:

- To determine whether the user can make payments with Apple Pay
- To present the payment sheet to the user

This class communicates with its delegate (which you implement) using the methods of the PKPaymentAuthorizationViewControllerDelegate protocol.

Determining Apple Pay support

The following methods determine whether the device supports Apple Pay and whether the payment cards that the user has added support particular payment networks and payment processing capabilities.

+canMakePayments

This indicates whether the device supports Apple Pay.

For example, to determine whether the device supports Apple Pay, you can use code similar to this:

```
BOOL can_use_ApplePay= [PKPaymentAuthorizationViewController
canMakePayments];
```

+canMakePaymentsUsingNetworks:

This indicates whether the user can use Apple Pay through the networks you support. If the user has not added a payment card to the device, the method returns NO.

You can call this method after calling `canMakePayments`.

For example, to accept only payment cards from Visa or Amex, use code similar to this:

```
BOOL can_use_ApplePay_with_Amex_and_Visa=
  [PKPaymentAuthorizationViewController
          canMakePaymentsUsingNetworks:@[PKPaymentNetworkVisa,
PKPaymentNetworkAmex];
```

These constants identify the payment networks that Apple Pay supports:

- PKPaymentNetworkAmex
- PKPaymentNetworkDiscover
- PKPaymentNetworkMasterCard
- PKPaymentNetworkPrivateLabel (this is for store cards)
- PKPaymentNetworkVisa

+canMakePaymentsUsingNetworks:capabilities:

This indicates whether the user can use Apple Pay on the device through the payment networks and payment processing capabilities you support (such as 3D Secure and EMV). If the user has not added a compatible payment card to the device, the method returns NO.

You can call this method after calling `canMakePayments`.

For example, to accept only payment cards from Visa or Amex that support the 3D Secure and EMV protocols, you can use this code:

```
BOOL can_use_ApplePay_with_Amex_and_Visa_debit_card=
  [PKPaymentAuthorizationViewController
        canMakePaymentsUsingNetworks: @[PKPaymentNetworkVisa,
PKPaymentNetworkAmex]
                      capabilities: PKMerchantCapability3DS |
PKMerchantCapabilityEMV];
```

These constants identify the payment processing capabilities that Apple Pay supports:

- `PKMerchantCapability3DS`
- `PKMerchantCapabilityEMV`
- `PKMerchantCapabilityCredit`
- `PKMerchantCapabilityDebit`

Initializing and presenting

The following methods prepare and present a payment sheet.

-initWithPaymentRequest:

This initializes an allocated `PKPaymentAuthorizationViewController` object with a payment request.

-initWithPaymentRequest:

If the user can use Apple Pay, this method initializes a payment authorization view controller (payment sheet) with the provided `PKPaymentRequest` object.

You can call this method after you configure a payment request.

Payment sheet delegate

This property identifies the object to which the payment sheet reports changes to the payment request:

delegate id <PKPaymentAuthorizationViewController Delegate>

This is the object that adopts the `PKPaymentAuthorizationViewController Delegate` protocol to respond to payment sheet user events.

The PKPayment class

The PKPayment class represents a user-authorized payment. You will get a PKPayment object when the user authorizes a payment request in the payment sheet (through the paymentAuthorizationViewController:didAuthorizePayment:c ompletion: method of the PKPaymentAuthorizationViewControllerDelegate protocol). A PKPayment object has the payment information required by your payment gateway and the issuing and acquiring banks to process the payment, charge the user's card, and deposit the funds in your account. This is also for your order processing web app to initiate the service or ship the purchased goods to the customer after the issuing bank authorizes the transaction.

Payment information

This property contains information about the payment, which identifies the payment card used, the banks involved in the transaction, and other details:

token (PKPaymentToken*)

This is the encrypted payment information used by the payment gateway, the issuing bank, and the acquiring bank.

Billing and shipping contacts

This property contains the billing and shipping information marked as "required" in the payment request used to initialize the payment sheet:

billingContact (PKContact*)

This contains the billing contact information for the transaction. Only the fields identified in the requiredBillingAddressFields property of the payment request are populated. If no fields are requested, this property will be nil.

shippingContact (PKContact*)

This is the shipping contact information for the transaction. Only the fields identified in the requiredShippingAddressFields property of the payment request are populated. If no fields are requested, this property will be nil.

shippingMethod

This identifies the shipping method chosen by the user from the list of shipping methods in the shippingMethods property of the payment request.

The PKPaymentToken class

A `PKPaymentToken` object contains the encrypted payment information used by the payment gateway and banks, the type of payment card used to fund the payment (debit, credit, or private label), and an identifier for the transaction.

Note that some payment gateway APIs do not use this class in their workflow. Instead, they provide their own payment token class. The example project, which uses Stripe, uses the `STPToken` class. Take a look at the `process_ApplePay_payment_with_Stripe:completion:` method of the `ProductCard` class (`ProductCard.m`) for details.

Encrypted payment information

This property is decrypted only by the entities authorized to do so, such as your payment gateway.

paymentData (NSData*)

This is the encrypted payment information for the transaction.

Payment method and transaction identifier

These properties provide information about the payment token.

paymentMethod (PKPaymentMethod*)

This is the payment method to use for the transaction.

transactionIdentifier (NSString*)

This is the identifier for the transaction that is assigned by your payment gateway.

Payment sheet user event protocol

This section describes the protocol used by the payment sheet to communicate with its delegate.

The PKPaymentAuthorizationView ControllerDelegate protocol

The `PKPaymentAuthorizationViewControllerDelegate` protocol specifies the set of methods that the payment sheet uses to communicate events to its delegate (which you can implement to respond to calls to these methods). The following sections identify the actions that the user can perform in the payment sheet and the delegate methods called when the user performs them.

The user chooses a payment card

The user can switch payment cards in the payment sheet (that is, if the user added more than one payment card to Apple Pay on the device).

-paymentAuthorizationViewController:didSelectPaymentMethod: completion:

This is called when the user chooses a payment card. If the payment card affects the payment request's summary items (for example, if you provide a discount to use a store card), you must compute the summary items (which are an array of `PKPaymentSummaryItem` objects) for the payment request. In any event, you must provide the summary items array as the argument to this method's completion handler.

The user selects a shipping address

The user can select a shipping address from a list of previously entered addresses or enter a new one in the payment sheet.

-paymentAuthorizationViewController:didSelectShippingC ontact: completion:

This is called after the user specifies a shipping address. The payment sheet provides the shipping address in the `PKContact*  contact` parameter. This shipping address is anonymized (that is, it excludes personal information). In the U.S., this information includes only city, state, and zip code.

If your shipping methods vary depending on the shipping address, in this method, you should create an array of the shipping methods that are available for the new shipping address. You should also recompute the summary item array for the payment request using the first shipping method in the recomputed shipping method array to compute shipping costs (the payment sheet selects the first shipping method in the shipping method array).

The completion block for this method takes three arguments: `status`, `shippingMethods`, and `summaryItems`:

- `status`: This indicates whether the shipping address is valid. If the shipping address the user specified is correct, set this argument to `PKPaymentAuthorizationStatusSuccess`. Otherwise, set its value to `PKPaymentAuthorizationStatusInvalidShippingPostalAddress`.

- `shippingMethods`: This is the recomputed shipping method array.

- `summaryItems`: This is the recomputed summary item array.

The user selects a shipping method

The user can select a shipping method from the list of shipping methods you support (this is stored in the `shippingMethods` property of the payment request).

-paymentAuthorizationViewController:didSelectShippingMethod: completion:

This is called when the user selects a shipment method. If the shipment method that the user chooses affects the payment request's summary items (for example, if the shipment methods have different prices), you must recompute the summary items (an array of `PKPaymentSummaryItem` objects) for the payment request.

The completion block for this method takes two arguments: `status`, and `summaryItems`.

- `status`: This indicates whether the shipping method and shipping address (specified in the call to the `paymentAuthorizationViewController:didSelectShippingContact:completion:` delegate method) are valid. If the shipping address the user specified is correct, set this argument to `PKPaymentAuthorizationStatusSuccess`. Otherwise, set its value to `PKPaymentAuthorizationStatusInvalidShippingPostalAddress`.

- `summaryItems`: This is the recomputed summary item array.

The user authorizes the payment request

After the user confirms or changes the information in the payment sheet, the user can authorize the payment request to proceed with the Apple Pay transaction.

-paymentAuthorizationViewControllerWill AuthorizePayment:

This is called after the user authenticates the payment sheet but before `paymentAuthorizationViewController:didAuthorizePayment:completion:` is called. Use this method to prepare for authorization.

-paymentAuthorizationViewController:didAuthorizePayment: completion:

This is called after the user authorizes the payment request. This is where you process the payment with your payment gateway. When done, you must call the completion handler block (`(void (^)(PKPaymentAuthorizationStatus status))` `completion`) with the appropriate value for the status argument.

These are the possible values for the `status` argument of the completion handler:

- `PKPaymentAuthorizationStatusSuccess`: This indicates successful payment authorization by the payment card's issuing bank

- `PKPaymentAuthorizationStatusFailure`: This indicates failure due to a failed authorization by the payment card's issuing bank

- `PKPaymentAuthorizationStatusInvalidBillingPostalAddress`: This indicates failure due to an invalid billing address

- `PKPaymentAuthorizationStatusInvalidShippingPostalAddress`: This indicates failure due to an invalid shipping address

- `PKPaymentAuthorizationStatusInvalidShippingContact`: This indicates failure due to an invalid shipping contact

The payment sheet is done

The payment sheet is done after the user authorizes the payment request and the app processes the Apple Pay transaction, or the user cancels the payment sheet.

-paymentAuthorizationViewControllerDidFinish:

This is called when the transaction is done or the user cancels the payment sheet. You must dismiss the payment sheet and perform any other necessary updates.

Auxiliary classes

This section describes some additional classes you must use to work with the Apple Pay API. The classes are:

- `PKContact`: This is used to represent contact information (name, phone number, and e-mail) and addresses
- `CNPhoneNumber`: This is used to represent a phone number
- `CNPostalAddress`: This is used to represent addresses

The PKContact class

The `PKContact` class contains properties that represent the components of a billing or shipping address. The payment sheet provides instances of this class to its delegate when the user selects a shipping address (`paymentAuthorizationViewController: didSelectShippingContact:completion:`), and in the `PKPayment` object it provides when the user authorizes the payment request (`paymentAuthorizationVi ewController:didAuthorizePayment:completion:`).

Contact address components

These properties contain the information requested in the `requiredBillingAddressFields` or `requiredShippingAddressFields` properties of the `PKPaymentRequest` object. The value of properties corresponding to the unrequested address fields is `nil`.

emailAddress (NSString*)

This is the contact's e-mail address.

name (NSPersonNameComponents*)

This is the contact's name.

phoneNumber (CNPhoneNumber*)

This is the contact's phone number.

postalAddress (CNPostalAddress*)

This is the contact's postal address.

The NSPersonNameComponents class

The NSPersonNameComponents class contains properties that represent the components of a person's name.

Person name components

These properties represent the components of a person's name.

namePrefix (NSString*)

This is a prefix (or title) used in front of a person's name, for example "Dr.", "Ms.", or "Mr.".

givenName (NSString*)

This is the given name (or first name) of the person.

middleName (NSString*)

This is the second name of the person.

familyName (NSString*)

This is the family name of the person (generally shared with siblings).

nameSuffix (NSString*)

These are the letters added to a person's full name that provide additional information about the person, for example "Jr." or "Ph.D.".

nickname (NSString)

This is the familiar or humorous name used for the person.

phoneticRepresentation (NSPersonNameComponents*)

If specified, this is the phonetic representation of each of the other properties in this class, except `phoneticRepresentation`.

The CNPhoneNumber class

The `CNPhoneNumber` class represents the phone number component of a `PKContact` object.

Creating a phone number

When creating a `PKContact` object, to set its `phoneNumber` property, use this method to create the `CNPhoneNumber` value to store in the property.

For example, this code sets the phone number of a contact:

```
PKContact contact= [PKContact new];
contact.phoneNumber=
   [CNPhoneNumber phoneNumberWithStringValue: @"678-555-1234"];
```

+phoneNumberWithStringValue:

This creates a phone number component with the text provided.

Phone number string

This property contains a string representing the contact's phone number.

stringValue (NSString*)

This is the text representing the phone number.

The CNPostalAddress class

The `CNPostalAddress` class represents the postal address component of a `PKContact` object.

Postal address components

These properties represent the components of an address.

street (NSString*)

This is the street address for the contact.

city (NSString*)

This is the city where the contact is located.

state (NSString*)

This is the state where the contact is located.

postalCode (NSString*)

This is the postal (or zip) code on which the contact is located.

country (NSString*)

This is the country where the contact is located.

ISOCountryCode (NSString*)

This is the ISO 3166 country code for the country property.

Summary

This chapter described most of the classes you have to work with to process Apple Pay payments. It also described the protocol used by the payment sheet to communicate user actions to its delegate so that you can respond appropriately. Finally, the chapter listed a few additional classes that you must work with to access address components, such as a person's name, phone number, and postal address.

This is the end of *Apple Pay Essentials*, conceived to help you add Apple Pay support to your apps. This book introduced the world of online payments, describing how payment associations, payment gateways, and banks work together to transfer funds from a customer's payment card to a merchant's account. Apple Pay improves on this model by adding convenience, privacy, and security to the process.

You learned about using the REST API in your client app to communicate with server web apps that provide the information that the app needs (such as details about the products you have for sale and the shipping methods you support), and to process payments and orders from the app.

The book provided an example workflow for displaying product information to your customers and displaying an **Apple Pay** button when appropriate. You learned how to create a payment request and add payment and order information to it, and to present the main Apple Pay user interface and the payment sheet. The book showed how to respond to the changes that the user makes in the payment sheet, such as selecting a different payment card, shipping address, or shipping method.

You learned how to process payment and order information in your app and backend servers after the user authorizes the payment request. The book also showed how to dispose of the payment sheet when the transaction is complete.

Finally, the book described the major elements and processes of an order management system, using `Node.js` to process orders and payments and the Mongoose module to interact with a document-based database.

With this knowledge, you are now able to provide the users of your apps with the convenience and security of Apple Pay-based payments.

Index

R

Representational State Transfer (REST) 12
required address fields, PKPaymentRequest
    class
  requiredBillingAddressFields
      (PKAddressField) 74
  requiredShippingAddressFields
      (PKAddressField) 74

S

secure communication
  implementing 67
shipping and billing information
  addresses, requiring 26
  addresses, specifying 26
  requiring 25
  shipping information, obtaining 16-18
  shipping methods, specifying 27
ShippingMethod collection 62
shipping methods, PKPaymentRequest
    class
  about 75
  shippingMethods
      (NSArray<PKShippingMethod*>*) 75
shipping type, PKPaymentRequest class
  about 75
  PKShippingTypeDelivery 75
  PKShippingTypeServicePickup 75
  PKShippingTypeShipping 75
  PKShippingTypeStorePickup 75

summary item, PKPaymentSummaryItem
    class
  +summaryItemWithLabel*amount
      type* 76
  +summaryItemWithLabel*amount* 76
  amount (NSDecimalNumber*) 77
  creating 76
  label (NSString*) component 77
  type (PKPaymentSummaryItemType) 77
summary items
  computing, for shared method
      implementation 36, 37
  specifying 29, 30

U

Uniform Resource Identifier (URI) 14
user interactions, with payment sheet
  payment request, authorizing 40, 41
  shipping information, modifying 37, 38
  shipping method, modifying 39

W

web server 60
web service 12

X

Xcode project
  Apple Pay, enabling 9

Thank you for buying
Apple Pay Essentials

About Packt Publishing

Packt, pronounced 'packed', published its first book, *Mastering phpMyAdmin for Effective MySQL Management*, in April 2004, and subsequently continued to specialize in publishing highly focused books on specific technologies and solutions.

Our books and publications share the experiences of your fellow IT professionals in adapting and customizing today's systems, applications, and frameworks. Our solution-based books give you the knowledge and power to customize the software and technologies you're using to get the job done. Packt books are more specific and less general than the IT books you have seen in the past. Our unique business model allows us to bring you more focused information, giving you more of what you need to know, and less of what you don't.

Packt is a modern yet unique publishing company that focuses on producing quality, cutting-edge books for communities of developers, administrators, and newbies alike. For more information, please visit our website at www.packtpub.com.

Writing for Packt

We welcome all inquiries from people who are interested in authoring. Book proposals should be sent to author@packtpub.com. If your book idea is still at an early stage and you would like to discuss it first before writing a formal book proposal, then please contact us; one of our commissioning editors will get in touch with you.

We're not just looking for published authors; if you have strong technical skills but no writing experience, our experienced editors can help you develop a writing career, or simply get some additional reward for your expertise.

Mastering Apple Aperture

ISBN: 978-1-84969-356-1   Paperback: 264 pages

Master the art of enhancing, organizing, exporting, and printing your photos using Apple Aperture

1. Learn how to use the advanced features of Apple Aperture.

2. Become well-versed with advanced topics such as curves and how raw conversion works.

3. Written in an easy-to-follow conversational style and packed with tips and tricks for optimizing your workflow.

Apple Motion 5 Cookbook

ISBN: 978-1-84969-380-6   Paperback: 416 pages

Over 110 recipes to build simple and complex motion graphics in the blink of an eye

1. Easy to follow hands-on instructions that simplifies the learning process to make it easy and effective.

2. Lots of in-depth information for FCPX users looking to integrate more Motion Graphics into their projects.

3. Learn keyboard shortcuts that will save you hours, if not days and navigate Motion's interface like an expert.

Please check **www.PacktPub.com** for information on our titles

PUBLISHING

Instant Apple Configurator How-to

ISBN: 978-1-84969-406-3   Paperback: 88 pages

Gain full control and complete security when managing mobile iOS devices in mass deployments

1. Configure group settings to personalise and secure.

2. Deploy multiple profiles.

3. Upload and manage Mass applications swiftly and easily.

Application Development with Swift

ISBN: 978-1-78528-817-3   Paperback: 144 pages

Develop highly efficient and appealing iOS applications using the Swift language

1. Develop a series of applications with Swift using the development kits and new/updated APIs.

2. Use the new features of iOS 8 to add new flavor to your applications.

3. A hands-on guide with detailed code snippets to aid you in developing powerful Swift applications.

Please check **www.PacktPub.com** for information on our titles